SUCCESSFUL CREDIT CONTROL

ROGER MASON

HAWKSMERE

© 1992 Roger Mason

Published by Hawksmere Ltd
12-18 Grosvenor Gardens, London SW1W 0DH

British Library Cataloguing in Publication Data

Mason, Roger
Successful credit control.
I. Title
658.880941

ISBN 1 85418 095 9

Printed in Great Britain by Ashford Colour Press

CONTENTS

INTRODUCTION

Research consistently shows that a typical invoice will on average be settled in a period between 72 and 78 days. A widely quoted survey by Intrum fixes the period at 78 days. As 30 day terms are normal the extra 42 or 48 days have a significant effect on profit and can represent the difference between a profit and a loss. It can even be the critical factor affecting a company's survival. To quote a phrase that appears in the book, "there is no profit until the money is in the bank".

Surveys also show that Britain's record is one of the worst in Europe. Foreign managers coming to work here sometimes find that a cultural adjustment has to be made. The British have all too often attached relatively low importance to credit control. In many, though by no means all, companies the people doing this vital job have not had the consistent support of top management, or of their colleagues in other departments. As a result the job has not always carried the status that it deserves.

The good news is that these attitudes are rapidly changing for the better, though there is still some way to go. The importance of the job is now more appreciated and professional attitudes are becoming more common. I can supply much anecdotal evidence to support this. A straw in the wind is that as a Finance Director I am approached for credit references much more frequently than a few years ago.

This book is intended to help everyone whose job includes responsibility for collecting money from customers. It is designed for the small businessman, as well as specialist credit staff, and also for those who would just like to increase their knowledge of the subject. I hope that you will want to read all of it, though you can if you wish just pick the chapters that are most relevant to you.

You should not of course follow every piece of advice given. If you do you will finish up with superb credit control and very little business. It is better to treat it as a menu, look at everything on offer and select the bits that suit your business and you. It is quite likely that just one idea will justify the time that you have spent reading the book.

Parts of the book are written in the first person and are addressed to "you". This is because I draw heavily on personal experience in credit control and my experience in presenting seminars on the subject. This personal experience will I hope result in very practical advice. I practice much of what I recommend, though of course not all.

Finally, I use "he" throughout rather than "he or she". This is purely for convenience and to avoid qualifying nearly every paragraph. Some parts of the book assume a company and a departmental structure. Much of business is like that but it is the ideas that are important. Most of them can be implemented just as well in a small business. I wish everyone who reads this book success in improving their credit control.

Roger Mason

1

THE TRUE COST OF CREDIT

It is interesting to work out the true cost of credit but there are very practical reasons why you should have the information at your fingertips. The knowledge will help you evaluate whether alternative courses of action are worth pursuing.

How much business would you lose if you did not give credit at all? Would the profit on this lost business be more or less than the cost of the credit? You will probably spend money to get the debts collected more quickly. How much money and is it more or less than the money that you will save?

Vigorous collection policies may cost sales (or so you may be told). How many sales and is the profit on these sales more or less than the cost of the credit?

Let us say that it is 2 pm on a Friday. The use of a motorbike despatch rider would mean that you could collect a cheque and get it into your bank that day. Would the cost of doing it be more or less than the money saved?

The Three Measurable Elements of the Cost

The following elements can be precisely calculated:

1. Interest Paid or Not Received

Most businesses operate with an overdraft and the rate of interest paid to the bank is a key element of the cost of credit. There is still a loss if the business does not have an overdraft. This is because it will be losing the interest it would have received through having the money in a deposit account or otherwise invested.

Let us consider a business paying 13% on money borrowed. Every £100,000 borrowed will cost £35.61 per day, £250.00 per week, and £1,083.33 per month in bank interest. The calculation for a day is

$$\frac{£100,000 \times 13\%}{365} = £35.61$$

2. Depreciating Currency

Due to inflation money banked after a period of credit does not have the same purchasing power as money banked at the time of delivery of the goods.

Let us return to the same £100,000 invoice and assume that inflation is 6% p.a. Depreciating currency will cost £16.43 per day, £115.38 per week, and £500.00 per month. The calculation for a day is

$$\frac{£100,000 \times 6\%}{365} = £16.43$$

3. Financing VAT

Some businesses pay VAT based on cash receipts, but most pay quarterly on fixed dates and with reference to invoiced sales, whether paid or not. For example all invoices dated between January 1st and March 31st will contribute to a VAT payment due to Customs and Excise by April 30th.

On average VAT is payable 75 days after raising a VAT invoice. It is tempting, but of course wrong, to say that nothing is lost provided that the money is received before the VAT payment is due. A day's interest saved is always a day's interest saved. If you can get paid in three days instead of four, the one day saved is worth exactly the same as the one day saved from seventy six to seventy five.

Let us return to our £100,000 invoice. It will probably carry 17.5% VAT and be for a total of £117,500. Assuming a 13% borrowing rate, each day's improvement in payment will save £6.23. The calculation is

$$\frac{£117,500 \times 13\%}{365}$$

The change in the VAT rate from 15% to 17.5% has increased the importance of this element of the calculation.

The Other Elements of the Cost

The following are difficult, or impossible to measure, but they are very real and should not be overlooked.

1. Cost of Administration

You will have to send out statements, make telephone calls and write letters, administer a sales ledger, deal with auditors, and so on. Probably the highest cost of all is management time. Many people underestimate the true cost of administration.

2. Increased Risk of Bad Debts

Studies confirm the relationship between the age of a debt and the tendency for it to turn into a loss. The fact that a debt is overdue may indicate that a customer has a problem paying. It may also of course indicate that he does not want to pay or that there is some administrative problem holding up payment.

A customer may be sound at the time of delivery and sound at the limit of the agreed credit term. But a change in fortunes may cause a problem after this period.

Remember also that if there is continuous trading the loss will be greater if a long period of credit is allowed and the customer then fails. If the trade is £1,000 a month, the loss cannot be more than £1,000 if 30 days credit is enforced. If six months credit is permitted then the maximum loss is £6,000.

3. Business Failure

In extreme cases the very survival of the can be at stake. Problems with liquidity and cash flow can cause businesses to fold, sometimes even profitable businesses. This is potentially the highest cost of all the elements.

You will probably know of at least one rather bitter person whose potentially successful business failed, either because of bad debts or because his customers took too long to pay. His business may well have been undercapitalised but nevertheless his credit control procedures probably contributed to the failure. If he had been able to solve the problem his business could have been saved. Such unfortunate people usually learn the lessons and get it right if they are able to start up again. How sad though that the cost of learning is so high.

A Full Example

All the above is best illustrated by a full calculation.
> *Assume:*
> An invoice for £100,000 plus £17,500 VAT.
> The company borrows from the bank at 13%
> The inflation rate is 6%

> *Cost Per Day*
> | | |
> | --- | --- |
> | Interest per day | £35.61 |
> | Depreciating Currency per day | £16.43 |
> | Financing VAT per day | £ 6.23 |
> | | £58.27 |

The other elements of cost are additional to this.

Possible Savings Related to Profit

Quite startling results are often obtained when the cost of credit is compared with the net profit of a business. It is common for unauthorised credit to swallow up much of the net profit, and sometimes it can be the difference between a profit and a loss. Consider another example:

Assume
- Turnover   £ 6,000,000.p.a.
- Net Profit   £   400,000.p.a.
- Bad Debts (Deducted before the net profit) are 1.5% of turnover
- The average period of credit is 60 days
- The company borrows from the bank at 13% and the inflation rate is 6%

Let us assume that a new Credit Controller increases the efficiency of his department and that as a result the average period of credit drops from 60 days to 45 days. Let us further assume that his efforts reduce bad debts from 1.5% of turnover to 0.5% of turnover.

Please check the figures for yourself but you will find that Net Profit should increase to £507,500. The extra profit comes in the following way.

£	32,500	Bank Interest saved
£	15,000	Saving on Depreciated Currency
£	60,000	Reduction in Bad Debts
£	107,500	

The other elements of cost are additional to this.

The saving does of course depend on there being no off-setting costs, particularly in the area of reduced sales.

This Chapter and You

Before leaving this chapter you are advised to do the saving calculation using the real figures applicable to your own business. It is best expressed as the saving to be achieved in getting £1,000 in one day earlier. If you work for a large company perhaps you should make it £10,000 or even a larger figure.

Having worked out the figure keep it in mind as you read the book and keep it in mind as you do your job. It will help you get your priorities right. ◆

2

THE RIGHT ATTITUDE FOR CREDIT CONTROL

Generals throughout the ages have known that their troops will fight more effectively if they believe that God and the folks at home are on their side. This is another way of saying that soldiers fight best when they believe in what they are doing, and it is why an army of volunteers is usually better than an army of conscripts.

It is stretching the analogy rather a long way, but it is true for business as well. No matter how well he is paid and trained, a salesman will do better if he believes in the product that he is selling. Similarly a person collecting debts will do best if he believes that he is a very valuable member of the staff doing a vital job, and if he believes that the requests that he is making are entirely fair and reasonable. He should feel that his work is appreciated and that his bosses take an interest in it.

It is obvious to me that this is so and I hope that it is obvious to you as well. Nevertheless perhaps you find it difficult to get into the right frame of mind, or perhaps your staff need motivating. The best results will be achieved when the collector is feeling in a positive frame of mind so this early chapter is devoted to helping you achieve this.

If credit control is only part of your job there may be scope for doing it at a time when you feel at your best. If you always wake up feeling depressed and only get going after the sixth cup of black coffee, then perhaps you should be phoning customers from mid morning onwards. Full time credit specialists may not have this option, but perhaps they could do the paperwork first thing. The way that a person is feeling really does communicate in subtle ways on the telephone and this is discussed in more detail in Chapter 8.

I take it as read that having progressed so far with this book you are entirely persuaded of the importance of effective credit control. If the problem is with your staff I recommend that you take the following steps to improve their morale:

1. Tell them the amount of money per day that the business saves by having the money in its bank. This was covered in Chapter 1. It really does boost the ego to bank a cheque on a Friday and think that one has saved £90 (or some other sum) by getting it then rather than the following Monday.

2. Give them all the backing that you can. This does not mean that they are always right and can trample on other departments. It means that they are doing a difficult and important job. They should generally get your support

and your best efforts to see that they get the support of top management throughout the company.

Some people find it helpful to have truisms pinned up in the office. Others keep certain phrases in mind and mutter them to themselves when the customers are being difficult. The following are all true and may be helpful.

I am doing one of the most important jobs in the company.

Credit is not a right - and even if it is, extra credit is not a right.

We are not a bank.

We are not a registered charity.

We are not a branch of the social services.

We are not an agency of the Samaritans.

There is no profit until the money is in the bank.

The debtor does not belong to a protected species.

You have probably come across similar phrases that appeal to you. Mutter them under your breath when the going gets tough, particularly when you are subject to lies and abuse. In some circumstances it can be productive to say them to a customer, particularly if you can lighten the conversation in a jocular way. For example, perhaps you can remind him that 'we are not a bank' then offer an introduction to a good contact at Barclays.

Much of your time will be devoted to people who give you problems. Some will behave in a very unfair way and a few may be downright dishonest.

Do not go sour on the human race and never forget the customers who do not give problems. As well as being spiritually uplifting this is sound practical advice. It normally pays to be friendly on the telephone, at least to start with. So remember that most of your customers are very nice people, rather like you in fact.

One or two customers may pay early and some will pay on time. Quite a lot will pay shortly past the due date, even without being asked. Of the remainder a few are probably rogues but the others may have very sad difficulties with their businesses. Several may be at risk of going out of business and perhaps even their houses and personal assets are at stake.

Bonuses and Commission for Credit Staff

In many companies credit staff do a job where results can be precisely measured, and are closely linked to the efforts of identified individuals. These conditions may be suitable for the introduction of bonuses or commission for the collectors.

This is particularly true if the credit staff are collecting a large spread of small debts. In these circumstances luck and special factors play less of a role and the efforts of the collectors will most likely correlate with the results achieved.

As with all bonus and commission schemes the best results will be obtained if management remembers three golden rules:

- **Keep it fair**

- **Keep it simple**

- **Make the bonuses big enough to motivate**

In recommending these rules I write from personal experience. As a young accountant I was once responsible for a wages department that paid out bonuses on a newly introduced incentive scheme. The bonuses were very small, unfair and hideously complicated. After two payments I received a delegation saying that the people concerned had talked it over and wanted to save the company unnecessary work. Accordingly they wanted all the bonuses added together and given to a charity of the management's choosing. I did not devise the scheme but I have never forgotten the lesson.

Record your Progress

A visual reminder of the target and progress helps wonderfully to concentrate minds, especially if bonuses are involved. There are numerous possibilities but the golden rule is KEEP IT SIMPLE. The ideal is a chart that takes just a few seconds a day to update.

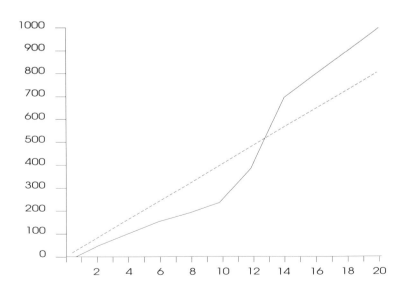

The preceding is a good example of an effective chart, and thousands of offices benefit from something like it.

The target for the 20 day month has been set at £800,000 and the dotted line shows how the money should be coming in. The solid line shows the cumulative total as the money actually arrives.

Staff motivation is likely to be best if the target is not easy but definitely achievable. Motivation also benefits if the target is set in consultation with staff and not just announced from on high.

Measuring the Results

It is highly desirable that you measure the results that you are achieving. If you do this you will be able to assess your performance and will be able to see if the position is improving or deteriorating. The monthly sales ledger balance does not in itself give this information.

Many factors influence an assessment of the monthly sales ledger balance and especially relevant are the monthly invoicing figures. A company selling christmas goods might have high sales ledger balances in October, November and December. This would not indicate poor credit control, just high invoicing in these three months. Quite probably a large part of the sales ledger balances would not yet be due for payment.

Many different systems are used for measuring credit control performance. Some are very sophisticated and have been developed to meet the precise needs of different companies. This might be ideal for special situations but for most readers of this book such systems are unnecessary. My advice here, as so often, is keep it simple. You should adopt a system that can be measured in just a few minutes a month. Whatever system you adopt it is important that you are consistent. Only by doing this will you be able to watch developing trends.

The most commonly used system is one that measures the average number of days credit outstanding. I use it myself and recommend it as a good compromise system for most companies. The system is best illustrated with an example:

	Net Invoicing	Net Cash Receipts	Net Sales Ledger Balance
February 28			£ 2,000,000.
March	£ 950,000.	£ 950,000.	£ 2,000,000.
April	£ 1,000,000.	£ 800,000.	£ 2,200,000.
May	£ 1,200,000.	£ 700,000.	£ 2,700,000.
June	£ 900,000.	£ 1,300,000.	£ 2,300,000.

The average number of days credit at May 31 is calculated as follows:

Balance at May 31	£ 2,700,000.	
Less May Invoicing	£ 1,200,000.	31 days
	£ 1,500,000.	
Less April Invoicing	£ 1,000,000.	30 days
	£ 500,000.	
Less March Invoicing	£ 950,000.	16 days
	NIL	77 days

The March calculation is £500,000. x 31 = 16 days
£950,000.

The average number of days credit at June 30 is calculated as follows:

Balance at June 30	£ 2,300,000.	
Less June Invoicing	£ 900,000.	30 days
	£ 1,400,000.	
Less May Invoicing	£ 1,200,000.	31 days
	£ 200,000.	
Less April Invoicing	£ 1,000,000.	06 days
	NIL	67 days

The April calculation is £200,000 x 30 = 6 days
£1,000,000

So in this example there has been a big improvement in June month. ◆

3

YOUR CREDIT POLICIES

Does your company have credit policies? This may sound flippant but some do not, except of course a wish to be paid as quickly as possible and this to be achieved without asking the customer for payment. It is sometimes interesting to ask the question of junior staff and senior staff in the same organisation. The junior staff often give a less flattering assessment.

At my credit control seminars I from time to time receive questions beginning "Why don't they?" The "they" are not the customers but the speaker's own management. This is leading up to the statement that credit policies should be very clear, and should have general support throughout the organisation. It does not mean necessarily that the Credit Controller should always get exactly what he wants.

Some credit departments are much put upon, but occasionally they do overstate their case. Sales really are very important and other departments have legitimate concerns as well. It is vital that priorities are balanced. Credit policies should be widely discussed but the final decisions should be taken at a very high level of management.

There are no credit policies that are right for all companies at all times. The point is that all the issues should be faced squarely and not ducked. Policies should be clear, should be reviewed from time to time, and should have the support of top management. The people doing the collecting then deserve, and should get, full backing. They should achieve good results and top management is entitled to expect that they do.

Credit policies should be realistic. It is useless to have credit policies not based on reality and such policies have a demoralising effect on staff. Credit control is a demanding task and the people doing it need to feel that they have clear guidelines and the support of their bosses.

The need for credit policies will vary from company to company but the following are among the points that should be considered.

Should you give Credit?

Please think very hard about this. If after consideration the answer is no the cost of this book is one of the best investments that you ever made. I always pose this question at an early stage in my credit control seminars and one or two people have told me in the first interval that they will think very hard about it and probably stop doing so.

Some companies give credit because it is expected, or because they always have, or because competitors do. These are all strong reasons but they are not necessarily conclusive.

I do of course realise that for most readers the answer is a definite self-evident yes. Nevertheless do consider the question. Concentrate on what would happen to profits as well as to sales if credit trading was abandoned.

What Nominal Period of Credit is Allowed?

This is a key policy. It will be influenced by the relative strength of your position, the attitude of competitors, the tradition in the industry, your need for extra sales, and so on. There are two cynical but practical reasons for making it as short as possible.

• Some customers will pay to terms, whatever they are.

• Some customers will take a fixed time beyond the due date, whatever it is.

What Actual Period of Credit is Allowed?

Whatever your collection methods you will assert increasing pressure at certain intervals. This will normally culminate in sanctions, usually cutting off further supplies and then legal action. In some industries, the supply of petrol to garages for example, the intervals are normally short and the pressure early and great. In other industries the intervals and pressure may be much more relaxed.

You should have a policy on these intervals and the pressure that you will bring. Special factors may alter individual cases but you will probably have standard rules rather like the following typical example:

- Nominal Term   30 days
- First Letter   35 days
- Second Letter   45 days
- 7 Day Warning Letter and stop supplies 55 days
- Pass to solicitor   62 days

Do you give quantity discount and if so how much?

This is discussed in detail in Chapter 10 on Conditions of Sale.

Do you give settlement discount and if so how much?

This too is discussed in detail in Chapter 10.

What Collection Methods do you use?

In most cases the methods will be a judicious mixture of letters and telephone calls and for most people the telephone is the method achieving the best results. However, other methods should be considered perhaps including collection agencies and factoring. If you have high value invoices and large balances with a customer it becomes more economic to have personal visits, messenger collection, and so on.

What are your Standard Letters?

There is a whole chapter on letters. You must have a policy concerning the tone of the letters, the number, and the intervals between them.

What are your Sanctions?

You will almost certainly face the problem of some customers being unable or unwilling to pay in a time acceptable to you. What will you do? Will you take legal proceedings? If so when, after what warning, and who will authorise the step?

It will be necessary to cut off further supplies. Who will decide and at what stage? Are there other sanctions that you can use? For example you might report a late payer to their Trade Association or Professional Body. A friend of mine recently threatened to report a solicitor's practice to the Law Society. The change in attitude was dramatic.

What is a Special Case and Who Decides?

There will probably be standard policies that apply to most customers but there may be some special cases who get different treatment. Perhaps a customer is particularly important because of his size or prestige. Perhaps there is a risk of bad publicity. In an absolutely fair world all customers would be treated equally but of course life is not really like that.

The Dominant Customer

This is an extension of the special case. Perhaps it should be called a very special case. It is a customer of vital importance, usually because he takes a large part of sales.

There are special dangers in allowing one customer to have a dominant position. You may be very vulnerable to the loss of his business and you may be in a weak position if he does not stick to the agreed terms. As a general business strategy it might be a good idea to try and avoid allowing any one customer to have a dominant position, though this may be easier said than done.

Permitting a dominant customer may be almost unavoidable. For example some defence contractors are almost bound to be in that position. A small supplier offered a major contract with say Marks & Spencer will have to think carefully about the implications, though that company does have a good record. Some other major retailers have a much less attractive reputation with their suppliers. .

It may be necessary to have special rules for a dominant customer and only permit approaches to be made by certain people. If things start to go wrong consider your position early. If you hold a junior position keep pointing out the risks to the boss. He may not like to hear them but he may be very grateful later. Over dependence on a dominant customer is one of the biggest causes of business bankruptcies and company liquidations. ◆

4

SOURCES OF INFORMATION

Good information is particularly important when a new account is opened. In time your customer's trading record will make you an authority on him and others will seek information from you. Nevertheless you should not neglect to get outside information later, particularly if problem signs are spotted. Your main sources of information are the following:

Trade References

A certain amount of cynicism about trade references may be permitted. This is because a company in difficulties may make prompt payments to two or three suppliers in order to maintain a supply of good references. There is also the possibility of fraud such as the customer writing his own from an accommodation address. My wife once worked for a company that was deceived in this way. The swindlers had a sense of humour and called their fraudulent enterprise "Conns".

Despite this, few companies do indulge in these practices and useful information will be obtained in a surprisingly large number of cases. The practice of taking trade references is undoubtedly on the increase. A Finance Director recently told me that the number of requests made to him has doubled in three years and my own experience supports this.

Giving a trade reference is an unproductive chore. It is only fair, as well as being in your interests, to make it as easy as possible. You should send a reply paid envelope and a letter that can be marked and returned in a minute or so. If you ask for an individually typed letter you are much less likely to get a reply.

For both trade references and bank references it is best to ask definite questions and mention a specific sum. A referee may in good faith give a glowing opinion based on his experience of granting £100 credit. This is all to the good but perhaps you have £20,000 credit in mind.

A distressingly large number of people seek references then disregard an unsatisfactory reply. If you are going to do this you may as well save your time and the cost of the two postage stamps. If a reference is unsatisfactory do not proceed without some firm reassurance from another source. If necessary seek further references from your customer and seek out information from elsewhere.

Similarly do not ignore failure to give a response. Some potential referees may not respond because they are afraid of libel, or because they do not want to let down an existing customer who may be a friend. No news is most definitely not good news and you should not ignore the lack of a reply.

It is worth trying a telephone call. Often the referee will be willing to say something that he would not put in writing. Even if the information is refused it may be possible to make a deduction from the tone of voice used.

There is no one best form for requesting a trade reference. However, the letter on the following page is a good example incorporating the points given in this section.

Circumstances will dictate the number of references requested. Many companies seek two trade references and perhaps a bank reference as well, and I would recommend this in normal circumstances. Do though ask for more if the credit required is particularly large, if you receive an unsatisfactory reply, or if you have any other reason for concern.

Example of a good request for a trade reference

PRIVATE & CONFIDENTIAL

Dear Sir

J R Smith Ltd of 2, Chiltern Street, Luton

The above has given your name as a trade reference. We
would be grateful if you would answer the questions at the
foot of this letter and return it in the enclosed prepaid
envelope.

Your reply will be treated in strict confidence and at any time
we will be pleased to respond to a similar request from
yourselves.

Yours sincerely

W Brown
Credit Controller

How long has the above named traded with you?

What is the highest credit allowed?   £

What are your payment terms?

Is payment normally   Prompt/Slow/Very Slow

Do you recommend them for total credit of £   Yes/No

Any other information that you think might be helpful.

Bank References

A bank reference may only be obtained using one's own bank as an intermediary and will be given without responsibility. There is usually only one bank so the customer does not have the option of selecting one that will give the best reply.

This is an advantage but the banker will only give an opinion on the account as he sees it. He will be commenting on the safety of dealing with his customer, not on the speed with which he pays his bills. A customer may be a very slow payer but still be well regarded by the bank. Indeed this may be the reason why he is well regarded by the bank.

The banker may feel a loyalty to his customer. He will not lie but he may put his opinion in the most favourable light consistent with the truth. Bank references usually need a little interpretation and many businessmen look at a reference and say "Yes but what does it mean?" Good phrases include:

'Undoubted' (this is the best reply of all)

'Considered good for your figures'

Bad phrases include:

'Fully Committed'

'We are unable to speak for your figures' (this is the worst reply of all.)

You may get a reply like:

'The figure is higher than we are accustomed to seeing, but the customer is a client of long standing and we do not think that he would enter into a commitment that he could not see his way clear to fulfil'.

This is a warning but you will probably be alright.

There is usually not much point in seeking a reference for a soundly constituted major public company. This is because you will be told that the customer is a soundly constituted major public company which you already knew. You will not be told whether it pays its bills promptly.

Trade Sources and Your Competitors

This is perhaps the most valuable source of information of all. Your contacts will be in the same business and may well be known personally. You will develop experience of their reliability and they will probably be receiving similar favours from you. They are likely to be forthcoming for this reason.

Many trades have a trade association or similar grouping which may be the basis of an exchange of information. In some cases staff will have friends and former colleagues working for competitors. It is worth making contact with your opposite number in other firms.

In many trades your customer is highly likely to have dealings with some of your competitors and the chances of obtaining useful information are therefore high. Such pooling of knowledge can be particularly valuable when the payment performance of an established customer is deteriorating. You will usually find that your competitors are experiencing the same problems. Sometimes a combined approach to the customer is the best way forward.

To get the best results:

- Do not abuse the network by asking too often.

- Do not tell the customer about the exchange of information.

- Be reasonably forthcoming when asked yourself.

•   Do not use the information to take an advantage over the person who supplied it.

Professional Advice

A variety of credit agencies provide reports on the status of businesses. The services vary from firm to firm and according to fees paid.

In some cases the information is purely factual, listing such items as directors' names, trading addresses, and key details from filed accounts and annual reports.

In other cases trade and bankers' references are quoted, and the credit agency will give its own opinion or credit rating.

Such information and opinions are often very useful indeed. However, you must be alert to the risk of the information being out of date or incomplete. A balance sheet is a snapshot at a certain date and it is due for filing some time after the balance sheet date. Unfortunately filing is often late.

The subject of credit agencies and professional advice is covered in more depth in Chapter 15. The use of credit agencies is particularly useful when trade references are not fully satisfactory.

Credit Insurance

It may be possible to insure some or all of the debts against the risk of insolvency. Note that you will be insuring against insolvency (or bankruptcy, total disappearance etc). You will not be insuring against slow payment.

The credit insurance companies make profits by assessing risk and making good judgements. They are very good at it and their opinions are worth a lot of respect. If you are refused insurance for a customer, or a high rate is quoted, then you should think hard about the implications.

If you have a good relationship with an insurance company you will probably be able to discuss individual problems. This advice can be very valuable.

Credit insurance is covered in more depth in Chapter 16.

Companies House

Annual Returns, Audited Accounts, Registered Charges, etc, have to be filed at Companies House in Cardiff. This of course applies to companies registered in England and Wales, different locations apply for Scotland, Northern Ireland, Jersey and so on.

It is possible to obtain copies of this information either by applying at Cardiff or one of its other offices. In all but a few cases it will be uneconomic to do it yourself and it is better to employ a credit agency or other specialist. Their fees can be relatively modest.

The information can be very valuable but watch to see that it is not out of date. Remember also that many companies disregard their legal obligations to file information on time.

Inhouse Opinion

You will best get the benefit of this mine of information if you cultivate an atmosphere where staff talk freely and exchange opinions. Do not complain if a warning in good faith turns out to be unjustified; the next warning may be vital. In particular it is important that the sales and accounts departments have a good working relationship.

Your salesman will have met the customer and may have been given a lead from another source. Maybe other staff have visited the customer. You may hear interesting comments such as:

'Not much stock about'

'A lot of staff leaving'

'They're desperate for us to take the order'

Such comments might not mean very much but they should prompt you to make further checks.

Your Own Records

Once an account has been established for some time your own sales ledger and other records will be a mine of useful information. In fact it will be so valuable that others will seek references from you. It is perhaps human nature not to fully value what is freely available and under one's own nose.

Your own sales ledger will tell you whether the customer normally pays to terms, and if not how bad his record is. It will tell you if he normally takes settlement discounts if they are available. Failure to take a worthwhile settlement discount is a very bad sign indeed.

Perhaps most important of all your sales ledger will tell you whether the customer's payment performance is improving, stable, or deteriorating.

At this point it is worth mentioning the "long firm", one of the classic frauds. It involves a customer establishing an impeccable payment record, then greatly increasing the volume of orders. It normally does this with many suppliers simultaneously, then closes down abruptly. Stock disappears and bad debts result. ◆

5

OPENING A NEW ACCOUNT

The actions that you take, or do not take, when opening a new account will send a signal to your new customer. If you take no action at all the customer will receive a very definite signal. A company that acts in a business-like way, and continues to do so when the first invoices becomes due for payment, is laying the foundations for successful future trading.

Most customers will respect a business-like approach and it might even improve the relationship. You may perhaps indulge in a wry smile at this point, because in some cases it will appear not to do so. This is a pity, but there is a lot to be said for confronting problems right at the start. If there are going to be difficulties it is much better to know rather than find out later when some damage may have been done and it may be harder to have things put right.

The role of the salesman is very important. At some stage it must be made clear what period of credit is acceptable, and what other conditions will apply. It is a matter of judgment whether this is introduced at an early stage or only after everything else is agreed. **BUT IT IS VITAL THAT THE**

CUSTOMER KNOWS AND AGREES THE MAIN TERMS, ESPECIALLY THE PERIOD OF CREDIT.

To leave matters unclear will very probably turn out to be a pyrrhic victory. The customer will then be in the driving seat and can say that his terms apply, especially his payment terms. It is usually more difficult to get the terms tightened than it is to set them properly in the first place.

Application for a Credit Account

Depending on the circumstances it may be necessary for the new customer to fill in an application form for a credit account. This will name his trade references, give information about the accounts address and so on. The form will list the terms of trading or refer to them. The period of credit should be shown prominently, and the form should say that this and the other conditions are accepted.

Frequently a credit application form is not taken, perhaps because the customer is substantial or well known. It is still very important that the customer accepts the terms, particularly the period of credit. They should be explained and then confirmed in writing.

You will probably have seen quite a lot of badly designed Credit Application Forms. This is very bad for the image of the company and it is worth spending some time to get it right.

Whilst writing this book I requested an account for car servicing at a major garage. The above paragraph was inspired by the Credit Application Form which looked like a poor photocopy of an original 1950s designed form. I completed it and was amazed to receive a two line letter, signed by the Managing Director, telling me that my application had been rejected. No reason was given.

I was both intrigued and alarmed. I am punctilious about my bills and to be refused credit is not a good recommendation for someone writing a book about credit control. I therefore rang the Managing Director and asked if he was willing to give me the reason. He gave me the very fair reply that it was garage policy to only give credit accounts to businesses or to private customers who had bought their car from them. It seemed a very understandable policy but the original presentation was a public relations disaster. Good credit control should help sales not upset the customers, at least not without good reason.

There is no single layout for a Credit Application that is best for all circumstances, but the following is an example of a good form.

EXAMPLE OF A GOOD APPLICATION FORM FOR A CREDIT ACCOUNT

To: J Perkins Ltd
14 King Street
Hertford

Dear Sir

We request you to open a credit account in the name of

_____

address_____

_____

We accept that all invoices are payable within 30 days of date
of issue. We have read your standard conditions of sale and
agree that they will govern all trading between us. The
maxium amount of credit required is expected to be
£ _____ .

Details of two trade referees are given below and we authorise
you to make the normal enquiries of them.

Signature_____

Name_____

Position _____

Referee 1   Referee 2

Name _____   Name _____

Address _____   Address _____

_____   _____

_____   _____

References

These were covered in detail in Chapter 4. They are often very useful and are appropriate in many cases. They have the indirect benefit of demonstrating to the customer that you take credit control seriously. If you take up references do follow up forms not returned and do not lightly disregard a bad reply.

Conditions of Sale

This subject is covered in detail in Chapter 10. The most important condition is usually the period of credit. This should be clear to both parties and accepted by the customer.

In this chapter it is necessary to stress that if the conditions are to be legally enforceable they must be part of the contract. Just stating the conditions will probably not be good enough, and it is certainly not good enough to print them on documents after the contract has been made. It is quite common for a customer to send a set of purchase conditions completely at variance with the seller's terms.

Ideally the customer should sign to accept the conditions, either on a particular order or on a document relating to all trading. Failing this it should be clear that your terms were last on the table when the contract was made. Whether or not the conditions have been accepted is a matter of fact in each individual case. In an important dispute a court would in the end have to decide.

Credit Limit

When you have completed all the checks that you consider necessary, and opened the account for the new customer, he is licensed to take deliveries and expose you to risk. Trading to a credit limit is a way of limiting that risk and it may be done for one of two reasons:

1. In view of the customer's modest requirements only limited checks have been done. There is a limit to how much time and money it is sensible to spend. Limited checks and a credit limit may be a realistic compromise.

2. The checks reveal cause for concern. Depending on the circumstances you may decide to take the risk, after all profits are made from business that you accept not from orders that you turn down. However, it may be sensible to limit the risk by setting an upper limit to the exposure.

It may upset the customer if you tell him that there is a limit and what it is. You may therefore not do so, particularly if the reason is that you have only run limited checks. If he wants to do more business you have the option of making further enquiries later and he may not need to know.

If your reason is concern about the customer's standing it is usually necessary to tell him of the limit. He will need to know anyway if you are going to restrict his supplies. It is only fair that the customer should know of the limit and have the opportunity to give reasons why it should be raised. This can be in your interest.

There is a further reason for giving credit limits. It can stop large losses from fraud or due to a sudden worsening in the fortunes of a customer. Take for example a customer asking for £4,000 credit. Your checks might show that this seems reasonable and you might therefore open an account with a limit of say £5,000. This would not restrict the expected trade and could be reviewed if the customer wanted to expand the business.

Let us now suppose that the customer wanted to take deliveries amounting to say £20,000, either as part of a fraud or because he could not get credit elsewhere. Without a credit limit these supplies may have been given. After all it is an existing account, perhaps not overdue,.

Needless to say credit limits are not set for all time. They can and should be reviewed. The act of reviewing a credit limit forces management to make an active decision. Even if the decision is to take a risk it is a conscious decision taken after reviewing the facts. ◆

6

INVOICES AND STATEMENTS

The politician Iain Macleod told the story of his asking for directions in a foreign city. He received the reply "If I was going there I wouldn't be starting from here".

That might seem witty but not very relevant to credit control, but the point is that if you get the foundations right later chasing may be easier and perhaps unnecessary. Good foundations include timely, accurate, and well presented invoices and statements. If you do not do this, getting payment will be much more difficult.

Take an Objective Look

It is very likely that you have become so used to the design of your invoices and statements that you do not see them objectively. Because you are 100% familiar with them you consider, perhaps wrongly, that they are ideal for your customers.

A short experiment will illustrate the truth of what I am saying. Please put your hands behind your back then describe the face of your watch. Are there twelve numbers or are there a series of marks? Is there a mixture of numbers and marks? If there are marks how many and are they of equal size?

You will almost certainly not get it exactly right. Yet you probably glance at your watch forty times a day, every day of your life. Invoices and statements are like that. You look at them frequently but may not really know them. Put yourselves in the customer's shoes and have an objective look.

Do the invoices and statements look impressive? Are they good for the image of the company? Do they demand to go to the top of the pile rather than the bottom? Do they give your customers all the information that they want, such as order numbers, delivery addresses, and so on?

Are they well printed on good quality paper? Ask friends for their opinions. Seal one in an envelope then imagine that you are a customer opening the envelope.

It is normal to put the trading terms on the back in small print, but there is one exception. The period of credit should be prominently shown on the front. Your customers should have no doubt at all about the amount that is being demanded, and the date on which payment is due.

Try spending a few minutes in the Bought Ledger Department of your own company, especially if it is a busy one with a lot of invoices. See which ones the staff deal with first and ask them why. They might not know the reasons themselves but they do follow subconscious rules. What happens in the Bought Ledger Department of your company probably happens in the Bought Ledger Departments of your customers. You may learn some useful lessons.

Timing of Invoices

It is worth going to a lot of trouble to ensure that your invoices are posted promptly. In many cases they will be launched into a bureaucracy that takes several weeks to approve invoices for payment. The approved invoice will then be passed to an accounts office that may take a week or more to post it to the account.

The same accounts office may make payments on fixed dates, perhaps only once a month. By posting your invoice three days earlier you may well be paid three days earlier, perhaps considerably more if the customer pays on fixed dates. You should post invoices daily and not hold them back to save postage with a bigger delivery.

Of course it is unfair for customers to hold up invoices in the ways described above. But who said that life is fair? Help yourself by getting the invoices out.

It is a general rule of credit control that it pays to start early. For very large invoices with short payment terms it may even be worth considering hand delivery or messenger delivery. If credit is costing £300 per day then £30 for motorbike delivery may be good value. Do not overlook the possibility of faxing an invoice with a hard copy to follow.

Dating of Invoices

You should normally date an invoice on the earliest date contractually possible. This is normally the date of delivery. There is no reason at all why an invoice should be dated the same day that it is typed and posted.

There is an exception to this general rule and that is when there is a VAT advantage in dating the invoice after the delivery date. Consider the following set of circumstances:

- It is July 7th.

- Your VAT quarters end on June 30th and September 30th (with payments due on July 31st and October 31st).

- Goods were delivered on June 28th. The invoice will be £100,000 plus £17,500 VAT.

- It is a safe, first class customer who pays by direct debit 14 days from invoice date.

There is a significant advantage in dating the invoice July lst (not July 7th and not June 28th). You will lose 3 days interest on £117,500 and if interest rates are 13% this will cost you £125. But you will save 3 months interest on £17,500 and this is worth £568.

This is perfectly legal. VAT law requires you to date an invoice within 14 days of the event that causes it. This is normally the delivery but it can be stage payments on contracts, and so on.

Watch out for this advantage at the very end of your VAT quarter.

Size and Frequency of Invoices

It is better to send small invoices frequently rather than save up for one big invoice at the end of a series of deliveries. The advantages are:

- Early invoices will become due for payment more quickly.

- If the customer is short of money he may pay some of the smaller invoices whereas he would not pay one big one.

- A dispute should only hold up payment of one of the invoices, but it might hold up the whole payment if there is just one invoice.

- It may be easier to get the customer's approval on smaller invoices. Larger invoices may require more approval signatures, and approval at more senior levels.

The Chief Executive of a major British company has made a rule that no invoices over £50,000 are to be paid without his personal signature on them. Quite apart from any wish to delay payment, it must be remembered that he is an extremely busy man, and he takes holidays. He also travels abroad on business, sometimes for two weeks at a time.

This man, who is a household name, will not thank me for giving you the advice but I am going to anyway. Send him two invoices for £26,000 rather than one for £52,000. I recently did this and they were both paid on time.

Full Details

Never forget that you may be dealing with a bureaucracy. By helping the bureaucrat you may be helping yourself too. Despite their image, bureaucrats often have very difficult jobs and they often respond very well to someone making their path as smooth as possible.

You are asking for trouble if you send an invoice to H M Government, Whitehall, London SW1. Similarly do not address an invoice to Ford Motor Company, Dagenham, Essex. You must give them a lot more help than that. It may eventually reach the right person and it may eventually get paid. But do not bank on it and certainly do not bank on it being paid quickly.

You will do much better if you address the invoice to the right department, preferably with a room number, and mark it for the attention of a named person. You should most definitely quote Ford's order number and expect problems if you do not. Needless to say the invoice should be accurate in every way, especially the delivery address, and claim what is contactually due.

If you do all that (and many do not) you can expect my old friends at Ford to deal with it efficiently. If by any chance they do not, you will be much better placed when you start your chasing procedures.

Statements

Some companies do not send statements, relying on customers to pay just on invoices. They justify this to themselves by saying that it saves money. They also say that some customers completely ignore statements and rely entirely on their own records. So they do, some of them, but in my view it is a false economy not to send statements.

They help customers reconcile accounts, ask for copies of missing invoices and so on. There are also audit and control advantages in sending statements. Some companies only pay on statement and will not pay an invoice until they are asked. This is monstrously unfair, but do not give them the excuse. Send statements.

The rules for statements are similar to the rules for invoices, namely:

- Post them as soon as possible after the month end, within the first day if possible.

- It should be very clear what is owing, how much is overdue, and when the remainder becomes due.

- Payment terms should be stated.

- The statements should look impressive, be logically laid out, and give all the information that the customer will need.

You may face the age old dilemma concerning the need to leave statements open in order to include all relevant information. In some systems it can take several days to get the last invoices raised, cash allocated and queries resolved. This is particularly true where there are a lot of invoices. It is natural to want to send out up-to-date, fully accurate statements. My advice is:

1. Look at your systems again. Is it really true that things cannot be speeded up? Perhaps you are dependant on your colleagues in other departments. If so make a trip to the Blarney Stone and try again to persuade them to help you.

2. Ultimately you might have to strike a compromise between speed and completeness. Individual circumstances alter cases, but perhaps come down more on the side of speed. ◆

7

LETTERS

Telephone calls are generally more effective than letters, but they are particularly effective when they are used in conjunction with letters. Individually composed letters are generally more effective than standard letters. Nevertheless the economics of collecting a large number of debts, particularly small debts, will probably necessitate the use of standard letters.

I am a strong advocate of the use of standard letters but I am realistic enough to acknowledge that a significant number of customers will disregard any standard letter. This will be so regardless of the timing, content, wording and presentation. It is nevertheless worth taking considerable care with the timing, content, wording and presentation because this will improve the response of customers who are willing to act on a request made in a standard letter.

One of the disadvantages of a letter is that there is no immediate contact with the recipient. You cannot look him in the eye as you can on a personal visit and you cannot ask a follow up question as you can with a telephone call. An advantage of a letter is that it suits some customers to have a piece of paper; the bureaucrats again.

Standard Letters

Word processors enable high quality standard letters to be prepared with maximum efficiency. They also enable letters to be personalised with minimum effort.

Whatever your system of standard letters it pays to vary the content and timing occasionally. This is because customers get used to them and get to know for how long they can safely be ignored. If your system delivers a final warning letter on day 58 a few customers will realise it and arrange to make their payments on say day 62. This will always happen but keep them guessing by changing the wording, perhaps going to just one warning before the final one instead of two and so on.

This is sound advice for all your collection procedures. Whatever they are and no matter how good, they should be slightly changed from time to time.

Many companies send two standard letters before the final warning but perhaps just one is appropriate for your business. Good letters incorporate the following points:

- As with invoices and statements they should look impressive. Keep them short.

- The first one should be sent very soon after the debt becomes due. The earlier you start the earlier you are likely to get paid.

- The tone should always be polite but firm. You are entitled to ask for payment. Do not apologise for doing so.

- Give the customer an opportunity to raise queries. As well as being good for customer relations you want to know the information.

- Letters should always be individually signed.

- You should ensure that your letter looks individually prepared, even if it is not. Do not duplicate or photocopy letters.

- The wording of a second letter should disclose that it is a second letter. It will lose some of its impact if the recipient thinks that it is a first letter.

- If possible, letters should be addressed to a named person. If you do not have a name use a title such as Chief Accountant.

- Do not use a phrase such as "Please ignore this letter if payment has been made within the last seven days". It looks weak and you can safely rely on the customer to ignore it in these circumstances.

The appropriate number of letters will vary according to circumstances. If you operate with very tight margins in an industry where very prompt payment is normal, then you will probably issue only one before the final warning. Similarly, appropriate wording will vary according to circumstances. The following two examples are typical of good, all purpose, standard letters.

EXAMPLE OF A GOOD FIRST STANDARD LETTER

J Jones Esq
Chief Accountant
Burns and Fish Ltd
38 Broad Street
Northampton

1 October, 1991

Dear Mr Jones

We notice that a balance of £264.24 is overdue for payment.
We are not aware of any reason why payment should not
be made but please do let me have details if this is the case.

If your payment is on the way to us please accept our
thanks. Otherwise could we please have your remittance
by return.

Yours sincerely

K Green
Credit Controller

EXAMPLE OF A GOOD SECOND STANDARD LETTER

J Jones Esq
Chief Accountant
Burns and Fish Ltd
38 Broad Street
Northampton

10 October, 1991

Dear Mr Jones

We cannot trace a reply to our letter of 1 October
requesting payment of the overdue balance of £269.24.

If there is any reason why payment should not be made
would you let us know by return. Otherwise as the
account is now very overdue we must ask for immediate
settlement.

Yours sincerely

K Green
Credit Controller

The Final Warning Letter

In some cases all attempts to get payment will fail. You must then either give up or take steps to enforce payment. This nearly always means legal action but a believable warning will often produce payment at the last minute. Unfortunately some customers will ignore all requests for payment and will only respond to a threat.

It is good practice, and will save you money, to issue a final warning before commencing legal proceedings. Such a letter should have the following features:

- By definition there is only one final warning letter.

- Do not make empty threats. If you do not mean it do not say it.

- Make it short and to the point, but still polite and still firm.

- State the exact deadline and the amount to be paid.

- State exactly what will happen if payment is not made. Do not use vague phrases like "other steps" or "we will be forced to place the matter in other hands".

In order to achieve maximum impact it is a good idea to send the final warning by recorded delivery. This does not imply any criticism of the Post Office and you would not normally need to prove that the letter was actually delivered. The reason is purely psychological. It concentrates the mind of the recipient to see the yellow sticker on the envelope.

For the same reason the final warning letter should be addressed to the Company Secretary if the debtor is a company, with a copy to the person directly at fault. This heightens the impact and it is possible that the Company Secretary will put pressure on his colleagues.

The following is a good example of a final warning letter:

EXAMPLE OF A GOOD FINAL WARNING LETTER

The Company Secretary
Burns and Fish Ltd
38 Broad Street
Northampton

20 October, 1991

Dear Sir

Overdue Balance of £269.24

We notice with regret the above balance is still outstanding.
Although we wrote on 1st October and 10th October we
have received neither payment nor a reason why payment
should not be made.

We must now tell you that we expect payment to be made
by 27th October. If payment has not been received by that
date we will pass the matter to our solicitors with
instructions to commence legal proceedings. This will be
done without further warning to you.

Yours faithfully

K Green
Credit Controller

8

COLLECTION BY TELEPHONE - BE EFFECTIVE

Telephoning is one of the most effective methods of collection, much more effective than letters and second probably only to personal visits. If there are only a few debts to collect, or if the amounts are large, it will be cost effective to use the telephone heavily.

If the debts are simple and all the information is to hand a collector may be able to make 15 or so calls in an hour, though he may not be able to keep this up for hour after hour. If the debts are complicated, and he has to get out information and answer queries, his progress will be much slower.

If there are a large number of debts it is almost inevitable that letters will play a large part in your system. Use of the telephone should be concentrated on the biggest debts, problem debts, and those most likely to respond to telephone calls. Very poor results will be achieved if you start at 'A' and arrive at 'Z' several weeks later. It is essential to deal with the accounts according to some system of priorities.

If there are only a few accounts it is sensible to spend a day or two telephoning each customer in turn. If there are a lot of high value accounts it is probably sensible to make available the resources for large scale telephoning.

Unfortunately telephone calls are relatively expensive, in manpower as we have already seen and also in telephone charges. It may be sensible to keep down the costs by making most of the calls in the afternoon, but on no account should this be taken too far. The benefits of getting the money in will usually outweigh the costs of the calls. If there are many calls to make you should start early and pack in as many calls as possible. Favouring the afternoon only makes sense if there are relatively few calls to make.

The results that you get will be influenced by the way that you feel when making the call. If you feel happy, confident, friendly and efficient then this will in subtle ways communicate itself to the person at the other end of the line.

If you do not feel happy, confident, friendly and efficient, then the following should help.

Rewards for Effort

There are a lot of rewards just for the sheer effort of making a lot of telephone calls and asking a lot of people for payment. This is true even if your technique is not as good as it might be and it is particularly true if you have a large spread of uncomplicated debts.

The more you ask the more you will get paid, and the earlier that you ask the earlier you will get paid. Experience may show that 60% of accounts get paid within 10 days of a simple first call. 100 calls will produce 60 cheques. If you can squeeze in another 10 calls then the 110 calls really will yield 66 payments.

The Unknown Effect

Your call may have consequences not realised at the time. It often happens that payment will arrive shortly after an apparently unsuccessful call. Perhaps your call jogged someone's memory, or someone had a fit of conscience, or they have a policy of only paying when asked.

You are in the Right

Never stop reminding yourself that you are 100% morally justified in picking up the telephone. There will be phrases that appeal to you.

* 'We are not a bank'.

* 'We are not a registered charity'.

Have one or two phrases like these pinned up in the office. At the very least say them to yourself. Say them to the customer in a nice way when the time is right.

Let us suppose that you sell a box of ten widgets. If the customer opened the box and found only nine inside he would quite rightly pick up the phone and ask for the missing widget to be sent round at once. You are entitled to do the same if the cheque is late.

Feel at your Best

The way that you feel may well communicate itself to the person at the other end of the line. If there are tricks that work for you and make you feel at your best, then use them.

Perhaps you feel powerful when smoking a big cigar. Get one out when you need to feel dominant. Some people feel in charge of a conversation when they are standing up. If this applies to you stand up and walk around the room. The customer cannot see you.

The Right Tone

It helps if you can get to know your customers as individuals.

- Try and be friendly most of the time.
- Always be polite but firm. Stay polite even when provoked.

Be Prepared

Your call will be more effective, and you will be much more confident, if it has been adequately prepared. At the very least you should have at your fingertips the total debt, the amount that is overdue, and the dates and amounts of the invoices making up the debt. You should also know if there are any unresolved disputes, and if there has been a history of disputes or slow payments.

Adequate preparation is very important but do not overlook the need to get the calls in. Do not prepare so much that you do not make enough calls. This is an obvious trap for someone hesitant who would really rather be doing something else.

Get to the Right Person

The right person is the one who can arrange satisfactory payment. It could be the Managing Director but he is unlikely to do so if it is a minor problem. It is better to make the first approach to a reasonable level of authority, say the Accounts Payable Manager. If you do not get the right results do not hesitate to move to a more senior level.

Do not worry about talking to a junior person, perhaps even a very junior person. It is not your job to worry about how the customer organises its accounts department. If a junior person can give you the right result then you should be pleased to speak to him.

It is best to ask for someone by name and to do so in a firm but friendly way. If you do not have a name ask for an appropriate position, such as Accounts Payable Manager.

The response may be that someone else deals with that sort of problem. This may well be true and you should accept the offer and talk to that person. You will have achieved your purpose and talked to the right person.

Dealing with a Block

Sometimes you will be prevented from speaking to the right person. Either that person will not be available or you will be passed to someone without the authority to help.

If this happens try again and keep trying. Do not take no for an answer. Say that it is essential that you speak to the right person. Say that you will hold on until he has finished his call. Say it again, still in a polite and authoritative way. In a high percentage of cases you will ultimately succeed, because you will embarrass or wear out the person who is blocking you.

You may get the response that of course you can speak to Mr X but unfortunately he is in a meeting, or has gone out, or has gone to the north pole via the south pole. If this happens keep trying, ask for a specific time when he will be there, and ask for him to ring you back.

This will usually work in the end but in a certain number of cases there will be an unbreakable policy of avoidance. When you feel that you have reached the end of the line:

- Leave a detailed and unmistakeable message.

- Put it in writing.

- Move on to your sanctions. (e.g. a 7 day warning letter followed by legal action.)

Think About Your own Company

It is worth spending a few minutes thinking about what happens in your own company, because the same may well be true in the offices of your customers. If you hold a senior position think about who manages to speak to you and who does not succeed. If you hold a junior position think about who manages to speak to the boss and who fails.

You will reach your own conclusions but among the people who succeed are likely to be:

- A person who asks for him by name in a confident and authoritative manner.

- A person who has some power, for example because he can cut off important supplies.

- A friend of his, or at least a person who already knows him.

Among the people who fail are likely to be:

- A person whose manner and voice are weak and hesitant.

- A person who appears not to be sure who he wants to speak to.

- A person with an unreasonable request or a request made at an unreasonable time, for example at 5.25 pm on a Friday afternoon.

You will probably have heard salesmen manage to make appointments by asking in a confident manner. Perhaps you are already blessed with such a manner. If not work on it.

Keep the History

You should prepare for a call and have a certain amount of information in front of you. You will be better placed if you, or your predecessor, has kept records of previous contacts with the customer.

Similarly you will be helping yourself and others in the future if you keep records of calls that you are making now. Keep records of:

• Names.

• Times when available.

• Customer's procedures (payment dates etc).

• Promises given and dates that they were made.

It is good to be able to say "You promised me a cheque some time ago". It is better to be able to say "On 10th April you told me that £3,700 would be posted first class by the end of that week".

It may be a good idea to keep a record card on each customer. Then you will be able to see a pattern and will be able to see if a customer is reliable and likely to keep his promises. If you do KEEP IT SIMPLE.

Make Your Call Effective

You will usually get the best results if you keep the following rules in mind:

- Be friendly if possible - but be polite anyway, even if the other person is not.

- Sound authoritative. If this does not come naturally to you, work on it.

- Be firm. Do not beg or plead. It is your money.

- Do not put yourself on autopilot. Some collectors say their routine like a gramophone record, and it sounds like it. Hold a conversation, not just recite a script. Each person is different to the last and different to the next.

- If the customer has a good reason for not paying part of the debt accept it, but do not stop pressing for the undisputed part.

- Be precise and talk about exact amounts. Do not let the customer talk vaguely about "seeing what he can do". Make sure that you both know exactly what is not being paid and why.

Handle the Conclusion Effectively

The conclusion should be a cheque in the post, but whether this is achieved or not you should both know exactly what is going to happen. Perhaps nothing is going happen, or something is but not exactly what you want. Whatever it is you should both know.

At the end one of you should say what will be done next. Preferably it should be the customer who says it because he will then be more likely to feel committed to it. Perhaps a pregnant pause will prompt him into doing it. If you cannot get him to say the words then ultimately you must do it yourself, perhaps prefaced with some phrase such as 'I am making a note of your promise that ....'.

Dealing With Rudeness

There is a well known piece of advice about "letting the air out of the balloon". If someone feels very strongly about something it is usually best to let him have his say. He will probably not be willing to listen to your point of view until he has got it off his chest. This most definitely does not mean agreeing with him or letting him walk all over you; it means letting him make his point.

When the point has been made consider whether there is any justification in it. It may be hard to be objective in these circumstances but try. If he is right, say something like "I am sorry you feel that you have had to put it like that but you are quite right. I'll get it seen to".

Sometimes you will find that the customer has got a point but that it is only part of what is at issue. Admit the point, but do not be deterred from asking for the rest to be paid. This is a very common failing. If one invoice is in dispute, isolate it and ask for the rest to be paid. If there is a problem with a large invoice say that you will sort it out but ask for a realistic payment on account.

If the customer is wrong tell him so in the best way that you can. This means putting your point fairly and constructively, but also firmly and politely. The best outcome is that you will persuade him that you are right. You might even get an apology though that is probably being optimistic. The next best outcome is that you agree to differ, hopefully amicably.

The worst outcome is that you make the point, he does not accept it and is still casting doubts on the marital status of your parents. If this happens you will have to bring the call to an end and consider your next step. Do not mind bringing in someone else on your side and perhaps on his. This is not weakness. The object is to get him to pay, or at least to settle the dispute fairly. If you can get a colleague to do that you will have won.

To repeat! A final word of advice. Whatever the provocation be firm, fair and polite.

Use Questions Effectively

There are two types of question:

1. To seek Information

The reason for asking this type of question is because you want to know the answer. An example is "Your cheque was due last week and it did not come. Can you tell me the reason please?" You really do not know the reason and you want to be told.

Beware of the customer answering with something irrelevant and if necessary lead him back to the point. Say something like "We did apologise for that and we did give you the extra discount. Can we talk about last month's invoice please? It is two weeks overdue".

2. To Lead to the Desired Conclusion

This type of question is one where you already know the answer and it is often put in a series. It is a technique well known to lawyers who lead witnesses up to the desired statement. The following is an example.

'Did the copy invoice arrive?'

'Is it in order?'

'Has it been signed off now?'

'Is your payment run this Friday?'

'Can I expect the cheque on Monday?'

Note the way that is done. Each question is reasonable and is a small step forward from the previous one. It is hard not to say yes to each of the five questions.

Electronic Assistance

Telephones and the accompanying technology are getting more sophisticated and various aids are available to help boost the productivity of collectors. One device rings customers in turn and only alerts the collector when it detects a human voice. If there is a poor connection or the line is engaged it moves on and tries the problem line later.

This saves the time and effort of dialling numbers and waiting for replies. The device can work progressively through its entire database, or it can operate according to certain instructions. Account names and details are automatically displayed on a screen as the call commences.

All this will undoubtedly result in more telephone selling calls arriving in the middle of family meals. However, the potential improvements in productivity for telephone collectors are self-evident. Economies of scale make it more worthwhile for companies with a large number of debts and many collectors. ◆

COLLECTION BY TELEPHONE - OVERCOMING REASONS AND EXCUSES

9

Most Credit Controllers can tell stories about the implausible excuses given to them. My favourite is being told that a purchase ledger was on a computerised system dependent on satellite communications. The Challenger space shuttle had been going to repair a malfunctioning satellite but due to the tragic accident the purchase ledger information would be unavailable for an indefinite period.

Such stories may be funny in retrospect and let's be fair funny at the time, but they should not stop you getting the right payment at the right time. You will of course encounter hundreds of more plausible excuses, and some reasons as well.

Like jokes most of the excuses and reasons are variations on just a few themes. An experienced collector will meet the same ones again and again. For convenience this chapter classifies them into five groups. The following will help you overcome the excuses and get the right cheque into your bank account.

1. Problems with the Paperwork

Examples

- Missing invoice

- No order number

- Delivery address not specified

- Lack of sufficient detail on invoice

Recommended Approach

- Get the customer to agree that apart from the unfortunate problem the invoice looks OK and due for payment.

- Establish that there are no problems on the rest of the account, and that other invoices (if any) will be paid.

- Say something like "Right. I'll get that solved right away. You'll get it tomorrow morning. It is overdue so can you promise me that it will go in Friday's prompt payment run".

- Provide the missing information, then ring shortly afterwards to check that the customer has actually got it and is processing payment.

- If payment still does not come, ring again and take a strong line. Perhaps move onto your sanctions.

Comment

- This can be annoying because customers' requirements may seem unreasonable. Nevertheless you will usually have to do the work and provide the information.

- If it happens a lot there may be faults in your own system. You will need to examine your paperwork and procedures to see if changes are needed.

- You may find some customers doing it again and again without good reason. You will probably not want to call your customer a liar, even if he is, but you could say something that hints that you know what he is doing. Say something like "Oh dear we have sent so many copy invoices. It must be a fault at your end. Would you please send me a thousand pounds on account and let me have the other thirty when you've sorted it out? I know its right, but if it isn't I'll let you have it back".

- Embarrassment can be a powerful weapon to use against someone pretending that he has not got documents. You might try ringing before the next invoice is due and saying "I want to head off a problem this month. Its due in ten days time. If you need a copy please say now and I'll get it to you in good time for the end of the month."

- If the customer makes excuses repeatedly it might be worth a more in sorrow than anger approach to someone at a high level. You could say that the continual problems are making it difficult to do business, and ask that in everyone's interest some attention be given to the problem.

2.Delay in Customer's Payments System

Examples

- Invoice not approved

- No-one to sign cheques

- Books with accountant

- Computer failure

Recommended Approach

- Get the customer to agree the amount that is due for payment and is not being paid because of the problem. If the problem is unapproved invoices ask for the remainder of the account to be paid at once.

- Give what help you can. For example if an invoice has not been approved due to missing information, then provide that information.

- Get the customer to agree that it will be paid immediately the problem can be overcome.

- Nag them! Make them groan every time the phone rings! Bypass the accounts department and nag the man said to be holding it up. This may embarrass either him or the accounts department according to which is actually holding it up.

- Nag them again.

- If there is no-one to sign the cheque say something like "There must be some contingency for urgent cases. How are you going to pay the wages this week? I see. Well can I have one of those cheques please?"

- Be imaginative. Be cheeky. If the books are with the accountant, offer to fetch them back. If there is a computer failure offer your own computer expert to come round and sort it out.

- All customers have manual cheques. If the computer has failed ask for a manual cheque.

- If the account cannot be reconciled say something like "Alan, that gives me a terrible problem and its not our fault. Can you let me have £5,000 out of the £5,200 and give me the rest when you've got the invoices approved? I know I'm right but if not I promise you can have it back within 24 hours."

Comment

- This is annoying because it is clearly the customer's fault. You should ask the customer to sort out his own problem and do it quickly.

- Persistence and embarrassment are strong weapons for you as the customer knows he is in the wrong. Admittedly some people have a very high embarrassment threshold.

- Try a jocular approach. If it does not work quickly then you would normally move on to a stern approach and consider what sanctions you will take.

- Do not believe someone who says that there is no way that a cheque can be signed. Provision for emergencies is always made. Ask what they would do if the electricity was about to be shut off. Then say that the electricity is OK so can you have the cheque that would have been used for the Electricity Board. If necessary make the point to a more senior person.

3.Customer Disputes Payment Terms

This can happen when there has not been any agreement on terms and each side is pushing to get its own version. Alternatively the customer may have accepted your terms and later says that he intends to pay on a different basis.

Recommended Approach when Customer has accepted your Terms

• Agree the amount and age of the debt.

• Point out that the customer has accepted your terms. If necessary provide proof by sending a copy of the signed contract, or whatever other proof there is.

• Tell the customer politely but firmly that a certain payment period was part of the agreement and that you must insist that the agreement is honoured.

• If the customer still will not pay, your management must decide what to do next. You will usually have three choices.

  a) Take steps to enforce the agreement. This could be the threat of legal action as a first step.

  b) Decide to give in and accept the customer's terms.

  c) Try and negotiate a compromise.

• If you decide to give in and accept the customer's terms make it clear that you are holding them to the letter of those terms. If the customer says that he pays on 60 days ring at 9.01 a.m. on the sixtieth day.

Recommended Approach when Customer has not accepted your Terms

• Agree the amount and age of the debt.

• Try and persuade your customer that your terms are reasonable, normal in the industry, etc. Your negotiating position will be stronger if you are a key supplier or the customer is particularly dependant on you.

• Without conceding anything get a firm promise for a certain date. Do not let them go beyond what they say their terms are.

• Your management must make a policy decision as previously described.

• This problem was anticipated in Chapter 5 - Opening a New Account. It is better to face problems when the order is placed. It is much more difficult when payment is due.

4.Customer Says that He Cannot Pay Now

Sometimes he will say that there is a cash flow problem. Sometimes he will be forthcoming with details and say when he expects to be able to make payment. Sometimes he will be unhelpful.

Recommended Approach

- Agree amount and age of debt.

- Try and get a promised date for payment.

- Try and establish if it is a short term problem or if it is likely to recur.

- If the payment promise is reasonable and if you believe that the customer is making a good effort to solve the problem, you might agree to the proposal. If so, monitor the account closely. If the promise is not kept contact the customer immediately and reconsider your position.

- If the customer will not give details or a clear commitment you will probably take a strong line and proceed to your sanctions, probably starting with a warning of legal action.

Comment

This situation should always be taken seriously. You have a worrying problem and judgement is called for. Personal knowledge of the customer, his character, and his track record is a big help if available.

Some customers do get through a bad patch and deserve support. Some customers have bad patch after bad patch after bad patch. Regrettably this is common and any Credit Controller will have seen the same names on his problem list again and again.

It may be that the customer does not deserve your support in this way. In that case move on to your sanctions. It is often remarkable what a customer can do when he has to. Remember that you are very probably competing with many other creditors. He who takes sanctions, and takes them first, may well be the one who is paid.

Your discussions should be with a senior person. You should insist on this.

Note on Wrongful Trading

This may be summarised as follows:

Directors may be disqualified and be personably liable for debts

If

they carry on trading when they know, or ought to know, that there is no reasonable prospect of avoiding insolvent liquidation.

There may be circumstances, if you think that the customer is being irresponsible, in which you should remind him of this.

5.Miscellaneous

Already Paid

This is either true or it is not and it can be proved or disproved. So prove it or disprove it. If a cheque has gone missing, or the customer says that it has, ask him to stop it and issue a duplicate. If the duplicate does not arrive quickly then take a firm line.

If the customer is right you owe him an apology. Do not forget to give it.

Cheque is in the Post

This is the oldest excuse in the book. It is sometimes true but usually is not.

Ask when the cheque was posted. After three days proceed exactly as above and ask for a duplicate.

Technical Fault with Cheque

This is sometimes accidental, but quite often deliberate. Examples are "post dated" or "words and figures differ". You could adopt one of three courses according to circumstances and the value of the cheque.

> a) Post it back for alteration and return. If you do that do not allow a long period before you follow up and press them to deal with it.

> b) Take the cheque and wait whilst it is altered.

> c) Bank the cheque. Ring the customer and ask him to confirm to the bank that it is in order to pay it. There is no good reason why he should not do this.

Alternative c) is usually the best. Depending on the nature of the fault you may have a problem getting your bank to accept the cheque. However, they will not normally examine the cheques closely and will probably accept it for clearance. It is best to photocopy the cheque and only ring the customer after the cheque has actually been banked.

If words and figures differ you should mark the cheque that you are claiming the lower amount and then bank it. The customer's bank will normally pay the cheque if the lower amount is claimed in this way.

If the lower amount is correct then no further action is necessary. If it is not correct but the difference is small then you will probably write it off. If the amount is not small you should ring the customer, tell him what you have done, and ask for the amount still owing. ◆

10

CONDITIONS OF SALE

Conditions of sale are rather like the fire instructions displayed in hotel bedrooms. For long periods they are not needed, but when they are needed they are needed rather badly. It is worth spending some time to get them right but fortunately this work does not have to be repeated too frequently. Do not forget though to look at the conditions if circumstances change.

In practice a sale is often not governed by clear conditions. This is either because no attempt is made to agree them, or because both sides have a comprehensive set of terms which each maintains prevail over the terms of the other.

The Legal Position With Terms

As a seller you will want to ensure that your terms legally govern the contract, but be warned that this is not easy. It is no good just accepting the order then printing your terms on the back of the invoice. The contract is governed by the position at the time that it is made. The invoice is issued after the contract has been made. Having said that, it is of course a good idea to put your terms on invoices, statements, delivery notes and other documents, especially order forms.

Best of all is a signed acceptance by the customer. This can either relate to a specific order or can be a general agreement for all business. Next best is to be able to show that your terms were last on the table when the contract was made.

If the customer signs an order containing your terms then yours will prevail. If he responds to your offer by writing with an order and accompanying his letter with a copy of his terms, then his will prevail. It is up to you to say that you are only accepting his order provided that your terms apply, and to get his agreement.

This can at best be time consuming, and at worst childish and bad for business. But it is the law and you should know the risks of disregarding it.

A Licensed Insolvency Practitioner recently revealed that he rejected more than half of the retention of title claims made to him. In a few cases the reason was that the wording of the appropriate clause was defective and did not match the exact circumstances. However, in the great majority of cases it was because the terms did not govern the contract. YOU HAVE BEEN WARNED.

Drawing Up The Terms

You could write the conditions yourself or more realistically you could copy someone else's. This is usually a mistake because they may be defective, may not be comprehensive and may not exactly match your circumstances. Some points, such as retention of title clauses, may be very technical.

It is normally essential that a solicitor draws up the terms. Make sure that he gives you what you want and does not take on a momentum of his own. Good solicitors understand the commercial realities and welcome firm guidance.

Maybe you want a short list of terms written in easy to understand language. If the solicitor then gives you a statement written in legal jargon, do not accept it.

The solicitor may point out that his terms give you protections that short simple terms cannot. He is right to point this out, and to charge for doing so, but there is then a commercial decision to be made. You and your colleagues should be the people to make it.

Alternative Approaches to Terms

You may decide to go for a short, fair, simple statement of the main terms. This will probably be good for customer relations and increase the chances of the customer accepting them.

The other approach is a long complicated set of terms loaded in your favour. This may be more difficult to foist on the customer, but may be more useful if there is a problem later.

Period of Credit

This is probably the most important condition. Most of the conditions of sale are theoretical and make no practical difference in most cases. The period of credit is not like that. It is always important and it is often the key condition. There is usually no point in fudging it because the customer will then use his own payment period.

Even if you do not bother with the other conditions of sale get this one agreed. Recognise that if you do not agree it you are in practice agreeing to the customer's payment period. Most conditions of sale go in small print on the back of the invoice but this should be the exception. Put the period of credit prominently on the front.

You will want the period of credit to be as short as possible but you must be influenced by the attitude of competitors, the tradition in the industry, etc. It is lovely to be a monopoly supplier or a near monopoly supplier, but not many of us have that luxury. Most suppliers operate in a very competitive market place and this has to be taken into account. The attitude of the customer must also be considered. The more that he wants extended credit the more he may be willing to concede on other matters such as price.

It is worth repeating the advice given in Chapter 3. There are cynical but practical reasons for making the stated period of credit as short as possible:

- Some customers will pay to terms, whatever they are.

- Some customers will take a fixed time beyond the due date, whatever it is.

Retention of Title

This is sometimes known as the Romalpa Clause after the legal case of that name. Without retention of title, ownership normally passes to the buyer on delivery. If there is a retention of title clause ownership is normally retained by the seller until payment is complete.

Retention of title means that you can take back the goods if you have a problem getting payment. In the case of a liquidation you can take back the goods rather than (if you are lucky) getting x pence in the pound. There are some important provisos:

- You cannot enforce retention of title against someone who has bought the goods in good faith from your customer.

- You cannot repossess goods that have been altered by the customer. For example if you supply leather you can only repossess the leather, not shoes made out of that leather. Timber used in building could not be repossessed if a building had to be dismantled to get at it.

- You must give full credit for the items that you take back (this includes VAT). You cannot say that the goods are not worth as much because they will be old stock.

- You can only get your goods back with the customer's agreement or by invoking the law. You do not have the right of forcible entry.

- According to the exact wording in the terms you can normally only repossess items identified as being unpaid. If a customer has paid some invoices and not others you are only allowed to take items listed on the unpaid invoices.

- You must be able to identify goods as yours. It may be obvious, but for some items identification might not be easy.

Retention of title only applies to physical goods It has no value to the supplier of services such as a Management Consultant.

In practice retention of title claims are often difficult to enforce and their value is reduced by the problems listed above. Stock taken back may be old, soiled, or made to customers' special requirements. Nevertheless it is a powerful weapon in the seller's armoury and the threat of its use can put great pressure on a slow payer. It an be of great value in the case of a business failure. It is worth careful consideration.

Settlement Discount

This means that the customer deducts a certain sum or percentage for paying by a certain date. A typical example would be 'Payable after 30 days or 5% settlement discount for payment within 7 days'.

It tends to be most effective when first introduced and when vigorously policed.

It can be worthwhile but is often avoided because of the following drawbacks.

- Some customers might have paid on time away.

- It can be expensive. In the above example 5% is being given for 23 days, which is equal to 79% per year.

- Once introduced it may be difficult to withdraw.

- It requires extra effort to monitor.

- There is always the tendency for the customer to take the discount without paying within the permitted time. Sales Managers will say things like "Are you really going to crucify my sales effort just for one miserable day?" After a while they may say things like "Are you really going to crucify my sales effort for just three miserable weeks?" It is a good question and you should answer it before you introduce settlement discounts.

Quantity Discount

This is sometimes known as Retrospective Discount and is the discount given at the end of a period as a reward for the value of business placed. A typical example would be 5% of turnover over £100,000 and it can be very worthwhile for the customer.

It is desirable to make it conditional on all invoices during the period being paid in accordance with agreed terms. It can be very effective to ring a customer towards the end of the year and point out that late payment is putting at risk the credit note for a whole year's quantity discount.

Interest

If legal action is taken and judgement obtained, interest at the statutory rate is charged from the date that payment was due. Unless provision is made for it in the conditions of sale, interest is not otherwise payable.

The charging of interest for late payment is relatively rare and it will probably be difficult to enforce in any case. Nevertheless the presence of interest in the terms may put extra pressure on the customer.

One possibility is to have provision for interest in the terms, but to privately accept that it will only be charged in rare circumstances. These circumstances might be liquidation or legal action being taken.

Miscellaneous

There are hundreds of other items that might be considered for inclusion in the Conditions of Sale. Each reader must compile his own list but it might include a minimum order size and the method of payment. For export sales your might for example want to specify payment in sterling to a UK Bank.

◆

11

LEGAL ACTION - PRINCIPLES TO FOLLOW

It is sometimes said that declaration of war is the ultimate failure of diplomacy. In the same way legal action against a debtor signifies the failure of your normal credit control procedures. You need to ask what has gone wrong with your vetting and normal collection methods. Was it bad luck or bad judgement? Are there any lessons to be learned?

Nevertheless any company having more than just a few credit customers will need to take the step from time to time. If you have a large number of credit accounts you should ask if the number of legal proceedings are more than an acceptable percentage. Perhaps it is part of your policy to deliberately run a certain level of risk. In this case a higher than normal amount of legal action is to be expected.

Should You Take Legal Action?

Legal action will cost money, very probably more than the costs that you will recover from the debtor if successful. It will also take your time, just a little if it is a matter of providing basic information for your solicitor or credit agency, and giving them instructions. If the matter is complicated it will take more of your time. If the action is defended it will take a great deal of your time, and perhaps other people's time as well.

You should only take legal action if you are satisfied on the following points:

1. All other reasonable procedures have been exhausted.

2. You believe that there is no reasonable defence or dispute. If there is you should try and solve the problem first. It may be cost effective to make a concession even if you think that you are in the right. Only in exceptional circumstances will you want to take on a defended action.

3. You believe that the debtor has the means to pay. Obtaining judgement is only the first step. You will then have to enforce it and actually get payment. This is frequently much more difficult and you will incur costs whether you ultimately get paid or not.

This may all be very worrying and may make you think that legal action should be avoided at all costs. This is not the objective of the warning, but it is intended to make you think things through before starting.

You should sometimes ask yourself if you are taking legal action for the money or the principle. If it is a matter of principle recognise the fact, and that you are not necessarily doing the most cost effective thing.

Having got the doubts and questions out of the way you are going ahead. Good! Lets see that you win. This chapter and the following three chapters are designed to help you to win judgements and to enforce payments in the most cost effective way.

Use The Full Extent Of Your Terms

The commencement of legal proceedings marks the breakdown of the relationship with your customer. You will not still be supplying him, and you will probably not do so in the future. If you do make future supplies it will only be with extremely firm understandings.

You have been let down by your customer and his goodwill no longer matters very much. This is the time to look at your terms and bill your customer with every penny contractually due, even if you would not otherwise have done so.

Examine the terms governing the contract and consider (among other things) the following.

- Charge interest if the terms permit. If you obtain judgement you will get interest, at the statutory rate, from the date that the payment was due. If contractual terms provide for interest at higher than the statutory rate then invoke the terms.

- Consider if absolutely everything has been invoiced. Maybe certain items have been overlooked or for reasons of goodwill you do not usually invoice them. Goodwill no longer matters so much. Throw in the kitchen sink and bill the lot.

- Consider taking back your stock if there is a retention of title clause in the terms. Retention of title was considered in detail in Chapter 10. You will probably not want to do this if you think that legal action will succeed and you will get paid in full. This is because if you take goods back you will lose the profit on the sale and you might be stuck with old stock. Successful legal action will get you the money which is much better. The threat of repossessing stock might frighten the customer into paying.

The Final Warning Letter

It is sad but true that some debtors will only pay when compelled to do so. They usually do not want the expense of legal action or the damage to their reputation caused by a judgement against them. For these reasons they will usually respond to a final warning of the intention to start legal proceedings.

The same response can be expected from a debtor who has got himself into a muddle. A final warning may well prompt him into sorting the muddle out. In both cases the final warning will only work if it is credible. The debtor must believe that you really will do what you say, and he must believe that it is the final warning.

An example of a good final warning letter was given in Chapter 7 and it is worth repeating the key features of such a letter:

- By definition there is only one final warning.

- Do not make empty threats. If you do not mean it do not say it.

- Make it short and to the point.

- State the exact deadline and the amount to be paid.

- State exactly what will happen if payment is not made by the stated date. Do not use vague phrases like "other steps" or "we will be forced to place the matter in other hands".

- Address it to the Company Secretary if the debtor is a company.

- Send it recorded delivery.

Who To Use

A large company may have an inhouse legal department, but more usually you will use the services of an outside solicitor or credit agency. It is worth a little thought to select the one most likely to give you the best results.

Some solicitors fit in debt collection work as well as handling all sorts of other activities such as conveyancing, matrimonial work, and so on. Many of these will provide a very good service but they suffer several disadvantages compared with the specialist departments of the bigger firms. One of the disadvantages is the need to take a series of steps on certain dates. A specialist department (probably with computerised support) may find this easier.

For these reasons it is often better to use a specialist department. You may also of course use a credit agency and information about these is given in Chapter 15. Such firms, if well organised, will use a computerised system to issue a warning letter (if desired) followed by a summons or writ, and all the other steps.

The use of such a system can be a remorseless juggernaut where you press the starting button and a cheque appears at the end. Failing a cheque the juggernaut will take various steps to try and get payment, and will probably do it all without reference to you. This is exactly what most clients want and it is a very cost effective approach. You should though remember this if your wishes change. You have to take positive steps to stop or alter what is happening.

If you use the County Court, you can do the work yourself. If you use the High Court a solicitor must be instructed. The prospect of doing the work yourself may seem daunting but it is within the capability of most Credit Controllers. They have after all got their jobs partly because they are good at administration, and because they are good with figures.

The main advantage of doing the job yourself is the saving on costs. You will also retain control and cut out a link in the chain.

On the other hand many jobs can be done ourselves but we still use outsiders. The Credit Controller could probably clean his windows more cheaply than by using a window cleaner, but nearly all office windows are nevertheless cleaned by window cleaners. This is because it pays office staff to use their time in other ways.

If you process a large number of small debts through the courts you will probably develop the speed and expertise to do it yourself. In most cases it will be cost effective to employ someone.

How To Pay

Establish at the outset the basis on which you will be charged. Many firms will quote a percentage of the money ultimately recovered, plus court fees and disbursements. There may be no charge at all, or only a very small standard fee, if nothing is recovered. The restrained claims of solicitors, and the rather less restrained claims of the credit agencies, often state "No Recovery No Fee".

The percentage is usually on a sliding scale, perhaps 10% up to £300, a smaller percentage on the next slice, and so on. The solicitors and credit agencies are of course banking on a spread of cases with a no hoper being balanced by an easy payment.

This method of charging can be an excellent idea, but think twice if you have a large uncomplicated debt with good chances of success. It can result in a large fee for very little work. You should ask for special terms for one like that, or take it to a different firm. Solicitors and Credit Agencies will not thank me for telling you this, but this book is primarily advice for the users of their services.

A Credit Controller recently passed a debt for £94,000 to a solicitor operating a sliding scale of charges based on money recovered. The solicitor's first letter achieved the desired result and a cheque for £94,000 dropped on the mat 48 hours later. Shortly afterwards it was followed by the solicitor's bill for £1,100. The solicitor could not understand his clients feelings and rightly pointed out that his efforts had achieved the perfect result and that the last case had resulted in a bill for £23. In the end they split it 50/50 and the client paid £550.

Stay In Charge

Books such as this usually say that if you appoint a solicitor you should always do what he says. I am not at all happy with this. Certainly you should take his advice on legal matters, but the same is not necessarily the case for commercial decisions. You know most about your business and it is you who should take these decisions.

You may decide that it is too expensive to continue, or too time consuming, or the risk of bad publicity is too great. Perhaps you come to feel sorry for the debtor (this can often happen and you will meet some very sad cases). You may want your solicitor or agent to follow a different line of collection, or to take payment by instalments.

People sometimes take the view that once a solicitor or agent has been instructed his judgement cannot be questioned. The case takes on a momentum of its own. This is nonsense. You are the expert in your business; you are employing a specialist and you are paying the fee. You should listen carefully to advice then take the commercial decisions yourself.

This may sound hostile to solicitors and credit agents but it should not do so. Many solicitors would give the same advice and would positively welcome firm instructions and guidance. You should encourage your solicitor or agent to give his frank advice (whether you take it or not) and of course accept that he is right to charge you for doing so.

Establish The Exact Facts

You will save time and money by establishing the full facts at the outset. Most important is to establish the exact name and legal status of the party against whom proceedings are to be issued.

It is a very good idea to send your solicitor or agent a copy of their notepaper if it is available. This should give the exact details and if it does not do so an offence may have been committed. For example a company is required to show the exact name, the registered number and the place where it is registered, and the address of the registered office.

It is very easy to make a mistake with these details, and if you do so it will cost you money and also delay your action. You may know them as Smith and Brown, but are they Smith and Brown Ltd? Perhaps the real name is Smith and Brown (Midlands) Ltd. You have to get it exactly right.

It is commonly believed that your solicitor or agent will require photocopies of all outstanding invoices. This is not usually the case and you should save yourself this job unless it is necessary. What he will want is the total amount claimed and a list of outstanding invoices showing dates, invoice numbers and invoice amounts. These details are required for the interest claim which he will be making for you.

The solicitor or agent will also want to know what the debt is for, but just a phrase will suffice. "Supply of lawnmowers" would for example be adequate.

If you are confident of your case you should ask that proceedings be issued with just this information. If a defence is filed you can work on the extra information later. If the case is not clear it may be a good idea to take advice before proceedings are issued.

The Danger of Delay

If you are having problems with a debtor it is very probable that you are not alone. You will be in competition with others and you may be at a disadvantage if you delay getting judgement.

It is often thought that assets seized from the debtor will be applied pro rata for the benefit of all creditors with judgements outstanding. This is not so. The money will be applied to the creditors according to the dates on which the warrants of execution were issued.

Let us illustrate this with an example. Company A obtained a judgement for £1,000 on 1st October and Company B obtained a judgement for £3,000 on October 2nd. The Bailiff seized good which might be worth £4,000 to the debtor, but realised £1,400 in a forced sale. Company B got its warrant of execution one day later than Company A. Company A will get their £1,000 in full. Company B will get £400. In fact it will be even worse because costs will have first call on the money raised.

This is a powerful reason for acting early. He who hesitates may be lost. ◆

12

LEGAL ACTION - PROCEED TO JUDGEMENT

Unfortunately the courts, or many of them, are usually extremely busy and this can lead to a lot of frustration. They are a state monopoly and you do not have the option of choosing private enterprise. You can though make certain choices about the route that you will take. You can either:

1.   Go for a Winding Up Order (in the case of a company) or bankruptcy (in the case of an individual). This is all covered in Chapter 14

    OR

2.   Go for judgement in the County Court or High Court. This is the route followed in the great majority of cases and this chapter deals exclusively with this.

Prior to July 1st 1991 the County Court only had jurisdiction for claims up to £5,000. The High Court had jurisdiction for claims of any size with no lower or upper limit.

You can now choose to start proceedings in either the County Court or the High Court and advice on the choice is given later in this chapter. If the case is undefended you will obtain judgement and endeavour to enforce it through the procedures of one or the other courts.

Since July 1st 1991 new rules have applied for the allocation of trials for defended cases.

• Cases involving amounts below £25,000 will be tried in a County Court, unless they are of particular importance or complexity.

• Cases involving amounts above £50,000 will be tried in the High Court, unless they are so straight forward as not to merit trial in that forum.

• Cases involving amounts between £25,000 and £50,000 will be allocated between the High Court and County Courts in accordance with certain criteria fixed by the courts.

The County Court

As the name implies there are a number of County Courts, each with an area of operation. Proceedings may be issued in the court that covers the area where the contract was made. This may well be your office and is probably the most convenient. Alternatively, proceedings may be issued in the court whose area includes the place where the debtor resides or conducts his business.

The Summons

This is the document to be served on the debtor (the defendant). It must give the exact correct name, the address, and in the case of a limited company the address of the registered office.

You need to say what the claim is for. It is not necessary to write a long story about this. A phrase such as "window cleaning services" or "supply of books" is sufficient. It was stated in the last chapter that it is not usually necessary to provide copy invoices to your solicitor. He will though need to have enough information to say what the claim is for.

You must state the amount of your claim and may add sums for the Court Fee and Solicitor's Costs. These will be scale fees based on the amount of the claim.

The summons will normally be served by the court posting it to the debtor. For an additional fee the Court Bailiff will endeavour to serve the summons personally.

Court Fees

These can be claimed from the defendant but are payable whether the case succeeds or not. The scale charges are:

Claim up to £300   -   Fee of 10p in the pound or part of a pound.Minimum fee £7.

Claim £300 to £500 - Fee £37

Claim over £500   -   Fee £43

The Debtor's Options

Having received the summons the debtor can take one of four steps:

1. Ignore It

This often happens. After 14 days you may apply for a judgement which will be given automatically.

2 Admit It

This does not often happen but when it does you can apply for judgement.

3. Pay It

This is of course the most satisfactory outcome. You can insist on the appropriate scale costs but you will not get interest unless judgement is entered. This happens quite often because many debtors will not want judgment entered against them. They will pay up when the summons actually arrives and you prove that you are not bluffing.

4. File A Defence (with or without a counterclaim)

The defence need not be detailed or substantial. It can be as simple as "facts are not as stated - money is not owing".

The debtor may admit part of the claim and file a defence for part of the claim.

If a defence is filed, and the parties do not reach some agreement, the matter will ultimately be settled at a hearing.

The Small Claims Court

This is part of the County Court and can deal with claims up to a limit of £1,000. Efforts are made to make it user friendly and its procedures are as informal and uncomplicated as possible. It is considered unlikely that the parties will use solicitors though they may do so if they wish. If they do use solicitors it is unlikely that they will be awarded the costs of doing so.

The Small Claims Court is generally considered to have been a success and to have made the law and justice more readily accessible. The £1,000 limit restricts its relevance to businesses collecting debts, but it has made the courts easier to use in cases that can be brought before it. Small businesses, particularly those selling direct to the public, are able to use it quite extensively. It can also be used by the public to make a variety of claims agains businesses.

The Small Claims Court is designed to be used by the parties themselves , so a plaintiff bringing an action for debt recovery should normally do the work himself and not use a solicitor. Having obtained judgment in the Small Claims Court payment still has to be enforced. This is covered in the next chapter and alas is no easier than for larger claims.

The High Court

If the claim is less than £5,000 the award of costs may be limited to the costs that would have been awarded if the claim had been brought in the County Court. If the claim is for less than £650 costs will not be awarded.

Area Of Jurisdiction

There is only one High Court and it has jurisdiction throughout England and Wales. This is an advantage compared with the County Court where there may be a problem establishing which court is the correct one to use.

The Writ

This is the document to be served on the debtor (the defendant).

Service of the writ is the responsibility of the person making the claim (the plaintiff). Service on a limited company may be made by taking or posting the writ to the registered office. Service on an individual may be made by post or by handing the writ to him personally.

If service of a writ is made by post a period of 7 days from date of posting is allowed before it is presumed to have been served.

The Court Fee

The Court Fee for the issue of a writ is £60.

The Debtor's Options

The debtor may

1.Ignore the Writ

If this happens you may after 14 days (21 days in the case of a sole trader) apply for judgement.

2. Admit the Debt

If this happens you may apply for judgement.

3. Admit the Debt but ask for a Stay of Execution

If this happens you may apply for judgement but not take steps to enforce it. Within 14 days the debtor must file an affidavit giving details of his assets, income, liabilities, commitments and so on. He must also make an offer concerning payment by instalments.

4. State an Intention to Defend (With or Without a Counter-claim)

If this happens the dispute, unless a settlement is reached, will ultimately be settled by a hearing.

Application for Summary Judgement

An indication of an intention to defend may gain time for the defendant. He may do this despite having a weak case, or perhaps even no case at all.

You may be able to defeat this time wasting tactic by an Application for Summary Judgement, also known as Judgement under Order 14. You (the plaintiff) swear an affidavit containing the details of your claim and that there is no defence.

The affidavit is served on the defendant and the matter is heard by a Master of the High Court. If the Master is satisfied that there is a prima facie defence he will give the defendant leave to defend the action. He may give leave only on condition that the disputed sum is paid into court or the leave may be unconditional. If the Master is not satisfied that there is a prima facie defence then judgement may be entered.

The Choice Between County Court and High Court

You can choose to bring a claim in either court and if it is undefended your enforcement proceedings will be in that court. If the case is defended it will be heard in either the

County Court or the High Court according to the criteria listed earlier in this chapter.

It is widely believed that justice for the plaintiff is speedier and more certain in the High Court, but that unfortunately it is more expensive. There is a lot of truth in this. You should consider the following points:

- Costs will be higher if the High Court is used. The Court fee for a claim of £600 is £60 and this cannot be claimed against the defendant. The court fee for a £600 claim in the County Court is £43 and this may be claimed against the defendant.

- The High Court has jurisdiction throughout England and Wales. There is no problem with issuing proceedings in the wrong court.

- The High Court is reputed to take a generally stricter line on enforcing payments. This is to your advantage.

- A High Court judgement is enforced by a Sheriff. He is remunerated by commission. A County Court judgement is enforced by a Bailiff who is remunerated only by salary. Sheriffs are widely regarded as having better records in obtaining payments.

- The High Court has no procedure for receiving instalments from debtors and passing them on.

Scottish Law

This chapter, like chapters 13 and 14, relates to English Law. The courts and procedures described apply throughout England and Wales. Scotland has its own law and Courts. There are many similarities, although the names and terms may be different. There are though differences.

Scottish law is beyond the scope of this chapter but it is worth mentioning that the Sheriff's Court in Scotland is broadly similar to the English County Court. The Court of Sessions in Scotland is broadly similar to the English High Court.

An important difference is that a Scottish plaintiff may be able to arrest funds before a hearing. To do this he must identify assets and give an outline of his case. It is a very powerful weapon but should be used with considerable care. Substantial damages may have to be paid if the case is subsequently lost. ◆

13

LEGAL ACTION - ENFORCING THE JUDGEMENT

An inexperienced collector may be forgiven for thinking that obtaining judgement constitutes victory. Unfortunately this is often a premature conclusion as you have not won until you actually get paid. You should restrict yourself to just one modest cheer and most definitely defer opening the champagne.

Judgement means that your version of the facts has been accepted, but that was probably not in doubt anyway. In only a small percentage of cases is there a serious dispute about whether or not the money is owing. Everyone knows that the money is owing and the problem is that the debtor cannot or will not pay. So although judgement is an important step you still have to actually get paid, hopefully with costs and interest as well.

This might not be easy. The debtor has not responded to your normal credit control procedures. He has not responded to the threat of legal action, and he has not made payment despite the reality of a writ or a summons. He has allowed a judgement to be entered against him with all that implies for his reputation. He either cannot pay or quite possibly will only do so if he is compelled to do so.

It may be frustrating to find that the court will adopt the role of neutral referee between the two parties. One might think that it would take a partisan role in enforcing its own judgements, rather as a criminal court will take steps to enforce fines that it levies. Nevertheless this will not happen. The various enforcement steps will only be taken if applied for, and paid for, by the plaintiff. It is not a fail safe system and nothing will happen unless you make it happen. You may have to be a detective, either by employing one or by acting as one yourself. The court will just see that the rules are followed.

The various steps that you can take will involve further costs, though if you are successful some of them may be recovered from the debtor. They will be payable by you whether you ultimately succeed or not.

Many debtors are unfortunate or perhaps reckless, but are nevertheless not out to exploit the system. Regrettably some debtors will do just that and there are various tricks available which may be used to wear down the plaintiff. One is to claim that certain technicalities have not been properly observed, particularly concerning the servicing of documents. Another is to try for endless delay by asking for postponements and varying of enforcement orders.

This is all very depressing, though unfortunately realistic, but let us look on the bright side. You have won judgement and for all its faults the law exists for you to get payment. There are a number of things that can be done to enforce your rights.

The debtor has gained time, but interest may now be running against him. There is a Register of Judgements and an unsatisfied judgement over £10 will be registered on it after one month. It will stay registered and open for inspection for six years, even if payment is subsequently made. The debtor will not want the inconvenience and indignity of having his assets seized. If this happens the loss to him may be much greater than the value they realise towards paying the debt.

The judgement may order the debt to be paid at once, or if either party has asked it may order the debt to be paid by instalments. Procedures exists for the debtor to be examined as to his means. This is done on oath and it may guide you towards the most effective means of enforcement. It may of course lead you to the conclusion that to try and enforce the judgement would be throwing good money after bad. The debtor can apply after judgement to have payment made by instalments.

The various enforcement methods can only be used in turn. They cannot be used simultaneously. It is therefore worth considering which is the best line to follow first. If the debtor has assets but a low income then it is probably best to seek a warrant of execution. If he has a high salary but few assets it may be best to go for an attachment of earnings order.

The following is an outline of the steps that may be available to you.

Warrant of Execution

This is considered first because it is the most commonly used means of enforcing judgement. A warrant of execution is issued by a County Court and enforced by a bailiff. The High Court equivalent is a writ of execution and this is enforced by a Sheriff.

The warrant enables the County Court Bailiff to seize the private property of the debtor and to sell it. The proceeds are available for the costs of the exercise and then to pay off the debt. Certain items may not be seized though there is an upper monetary limit on the restriction. Prohibited items include the debtor's clothing and bedding and the tools of his trade. Goods owned by a hire purchase company may not be seized and neither may goods owned by his landlord, friends, or members of his family.

This is often a real practical problem as all parties may claim that the debtor does not own goods that are apparently his. This may be difficult to disprove. It may be true or it may be a pack of lies. The problem is worst when dealing with an individual or small trader. It will probably be less of a problem when dealing with a company or large trader. Hire purchase though may still give difficulties.

The Bailiff cannot force entry to a debtor's home but he can if necessary force entry to business premises. The Bailiff may take goods straight away but the debtor may have the opportunity to sign a walking possession agreement. This enables the debtor to keep possession of the goods identified whilst he makes attempts to raise the money. It sometimes happens that this is the point where the debtor finally faces reality and makes realistic efforts to make payment.

It is an offence for the debtor to dispose of goods covered by a walking possession agreement. If the debtor does not make payment within a specified time the Bailiff may return and seize the goods. If it is necessary for him to do this he does have the right of forcible entry to the debtor's home.

The money raised may be disappointing both for the debtor and yourself. Unused branded goods may fetch a good percentage of their normal retail price. Things such as fashion goods and second hand furniture may only fetch small sums.

It is worth repeating that money realised goes first to pay the Bailiff's expenses, and secondly to pay the creditors in the order in which the warrants of execution are granted. This is a powerful reason for acting early, in obtaining judgement early, and in applying for a warrant of execution as soon as possible.

Attachment of Earnings Order

An application for an Attachment of Earnings order must be made to the court for the district in which the debtor lives. By definition it applies only to an individual in employment. It does not apply to a limited company, a partnership or a self employed person. The definition of earnings includes salary, bonuses, commission, and pensions. It does not include the state old age pension, disability benefits, or social security benefits.

The debtor is compelled to give the court details of his employment, his earnings and his commitments. The court may then make an order fixing the maximum weekly, or monthly payments and the "protected earnings".

The protected earnings figure is the amount that the court believes that the debtor needs to fulfil his reasonable commitments. The court will exercise its judgement and follow whatever line of reasoning appears appropriate in an individual case. The protected earnings figure is after tax and certain other deductions.

Let us illustrate this with an example and assume that Mr A's employer is ordered to pay over £10 per week and that the protected earnings are fixed at £200 per week. In a week when net earnings are £220 the employer will pay over £10. In a week when net earnings are £203 the employer will pay over £3. In a week when net earnings are £199 nothing at all will be paid over. If there is a shortage in one week it is not added to subsequent weeks when money may be available.

Attachment of Earnings Orders can be an effective way of obtaining funds. They are most valuable when the debtor earns reasonable money, has modest commitments, and is in stable employment. You might of course think that this is exactly the sort of person least likely to get into difficulties in the first place.

Unfortunately, Attachment of Earnings Orders have the following disadvantages which may be exploited by some debtors:

• The order only applies to the named employer. If the debtor changes his job you have to apply for a fresh order each time.

• The debtor may avoid the order by repeatedly changing his job, becoming self-employed, taking undisclosed payments through the black economy, or deliberately earning below the protected earnings limit.

- In some cases the level of protected earnings may be so high that little or no money is available. This may be a problem when the debtor does seasonal work or depends on overtime. It is particularly likely to be a problem with debtors having marital problems and extended families.

If there is more than one Attachment of Earnings Order the employer has to apply them in the order in which they are issued. This once again reinforces the advice about acting quickly.

Garnishee Order

A Garnishee Order will enable you to take the benefit of money owed to the debtor. It requires the person owing the money to pay you instead of the debtor.

You have to have details of the debt in order to apply for the garnishee order, and money that you obtain is kept by you regardless of any other creditors who may have judgement orders.

Garnishee orders are perhaps most commonly used to obtain funds in a bank account that is in credit.

Garnishee Orders may be issued by both the County Court and the High Court.

Charging Orders

This may be of use if the debtor owns stocks and shares, land or property. A charging order may prevent the debtor disposing of his asset, or it may be taken a step further and an application made for an order for the sale of the property.

Appointment of a Receiver

This is appropriate if the debtor has income from rents or is receiving money from a trust fund. The Receiver will take this money, deduct his fees and expenses, and hand over the balance.

Bankruptcy or Winding Up

If all else fails you might consider applying for the bankruptcy of an individual, or the winding up of a company. This is covered in Chapter 14. ◆

14

WINDING UP, RECEIVERS AND BANKRUPTCY

WINDING UP ORDERS

Winding Up Orders apply to companies, not to individuals or partnerships. Furthermore they apply to companies registered in this country. The English courts are not able to wind up companies registered in a foreign country.

Winding up is very often a voluntary process instigated by the company itself, but this section covers compulsory winding up instigated by a creditor. A simplified summary of the conditions under which a winding up order may be granted is if either:

a) The debt is at least £750 and the company has failed within three weeks to respond to a written demand made in the proper form

OR

b) Judgement has been obtained and enforcement has failed.

The cost of an order is £750 in addition to the other costs, so it is not a cheap option. On economic grounds it is only worth doing for debts of a certain size. Sometimes several creditors get together and agree to share the costs. From time to time creditors wind up a debtor company as a matter of principle rather than for reasons of cost effectiveness. This is understandable, perhaps even commendable, but if you do act in this way make sure that you are honest with yourself about your true motivation.

Pressure Exerted by a Winding Up Application

The courts will get decidedly cross if the process is abused, and they will not like it at all if you apply for a winding up order in a case where there is a dispute. Your solicitor will not like it either. Nevertheless, the courts will give even-handed justice. They really will give a winding up order against a multi-million pound major company if asked by Joe Soap the window cleaner, and if the facts support him.

Of course the multi-million pound major company is most unlikely to be actually wound up. It is very likely to pay the debt, which is the object of the exercise. The threat of a winding up order often achieves remarkable results in persuading a company to make payment. All threats should be credible but it is worth pointing out that the £750 fee does not have to be paid if payment is made before the action is taken.

The reality of winding up proceedings is almost invariably effective provided that the company does not wish to be wound up, and provided that it has the means to pay. You can rest assured that your case will come to the attention of a high level of management. You can also of course be certain that you will not endear yourself to that company, and that your prospects of future business will be reduced to a point somewhere between negligible and zero.

When all else has failed, the threat to wind up a company will often achieve results. Thousands of credit controllers have proved it.

In passing it is worth mentioning that it may be effective to threaten to report a foreign company to the appropriate regulatory authority in its home country. I once did this to a Swiss company and obtained a very different attitude. Obviously the effect will vary from case to case and from country to country.

Winding Up - Summary of the Legal Steps

- Written demand for payment must be issued to the company. If payment is not made within 21 days the court may be petitioned for a winding up order.

- Alternatively, the court may be petitioned if judgement has been obtained and enforcement steps have not wholly succeeded.

- A petition is presented to the court. This must give the required details and the petition must be in the required form.

- The court will seal a copy of the petition which is then served on the company. The creditor must file an affidavit in support of the petition.

- The petition is advertised in the London Gazette.

- The petition is heard by the court. If the company does not contest the petition it will not be necessary to give evidence.

- The court may reject the petition, adjourn it, or issue a winding up order.

Effect of a Winding Up Order

The company must provide a statement of its affairs to the Official Receiver who becomes the provisional liquidator. The directors are relieved of their powers, and the assets become vested in the Official Receiver.

If a company is actually wound up the assets are realised for the benefit of all creditors in accordance with the statutory rules. The creditor bringing the petition does not automatically get paid first, or even at all.

Wrongful Trading

Directors may be guilty of wrongful trading if they carry on trading when they know, or ought to know, that there is no reasonable prospect of avoiding insolvent liquidation.

The courts have to interpret the word "reasonable" but the law applies to all directors, including non-executive directors. It does not just apply to the Managing Director, the Finance Director, and those most actively involved in the running of the company. People who accept directorships for reasons of prestige, either for them or for the company, might do well to keep this in mind.

If the court decides that a director has been guilty of wrongful trading it may disqualify him from being a director for between two and fifteen years. Critics sometimes allege that the courts use their powers in an inconsistent way. Although insolvency was not involved, the failure to disqualify directors convicted in the Guinness case caused some surprise. A more recent case is that of the failure of Homes Assured. The Department of Trade and Industry decided to seek the disqualification of Sir Edward du Cann and other directors.

If wrongful trading is proved, you may be able to set aside limited liability and make directors personally liable for debts. However, this is a separate matter to disqualification and one does not automatically follow from the other.

Receivers and Administrators

The Insolvency Act 1986 revised the law relating to insolvency. It attempts to be fair to creditors, and to debtor companies. In particular it endeavours to give increased opportunities for companies with problems to sort them out for the benefit of all concerned, and to continue trading, again for the benefit of all concerned. One of the ways that it tries to achieve these desirable ends is for the company to be given a period of protection from its creditors.

This is all admirable but it will be readily realised that there are considerable dangers involved. Delay, administered by the incompetent, the reckless, or dishonest, can be very unfair to creditors. For this reason there are rigorous safeguards.

In particular the Act stipulates that the positions of Administrator or Receiver can only be held by Licensed Insolvency Practitioners. Prior to the Act there were a lot of scandals concerning the competence and honesty of Liquidators and others.

Particularly prevalent was the practice of the people involved being hand in glove with the owners of the company, and selling the assets cheaply to favoured nominees. Esther Rantzen, the press and others regularly nailed the abuses of "Hissing Sid" and his like.

There are still occasional problems but things are now much better. A Licensed Insolvency Practitioner has to have certain qualifications and standards, and should be barred if he does not. You can be reasonably sure that he will be honest and have an acceptable degree of competence. You may nevertheless be infuriated at times. This is probably because he has a very difficult job, and is being telephoned simultaneously by numerous people, all claiming that their problem should have first priority.

There is room for only an outline summary but a key point is that the Receiver or Administrator can be given a breathing space of up to three months. During this period no order will be given for the winding up of the company, its assets may not be seized, and assets subject to lease or hire purchase may not be repossessed.

Rather than a lengthy recital of legal points readers will probably appreciate some practical advice on what to do on hearing that an Administrator or Receiver has been appointed. The first reaction will probably be to groan and reach for the tablets. Your customer may be going out of business and you may be going to lose some or all of your money. To add insult to injury what money is realised may well be going to pay legal and accountancy fees, and then to debenture holders, and preferential creditors such as Her Majesty's Government.

Your next step is to put the tablets down and think that it might not happen this way though sadly it quite often does. Perhaps an acceptable scheme to save the company will be put forward. You will have three decisions to make:

1. Do you remove goods if allowed to do so by a retention of title clause in the terms? If you are an important supplier a decision to do this will probably prejudice the chances of continuing the business. On the other hand if you believe that the scheme has little chance of success you will want to do this. To make matters worse you will need to move quickly. Your property may be sold on, altered, or perhaps "go missing".

   Insolvency Practitioners are well known for being difficult with retention of title claims. Nevertheless, they are often susceptible to pressure especially if supported by a credible threat of legal action. They hate that. They will of course quite rightly resist a spurious claim.

2. The Insolvency Practitioner will make it clear that he is not accepting personal liability. He will though probably put forward a persuasive case to show that you will get paid by the company if you make future supplies. You must decide how much credibility this carries.

3. You must decide whether to use any "muscle" that you might have to get favourable treatment. You might not have any muscle but an Electricity Board for example can probably close a company down by deciding to throw a

switch. It may be rather unfair on the other creditors to act in this way but you may decide to give your interests priority. If so perhaps it would be wise to keep away from the local golf club for a week or two.

Bankruptcy

Bankruptcy, by definition, applies to an individual. It is invariably a harrowing experience for the bankrupt, and also for everyone else involved.

Many, but not all, bankrupts have been reckless or incompetent or both. A few may have been dishonest. Nevertheless it is an unusually hard hearted creditor who cannot summon up at least a little sympathy. Some bankrupts may have been unlucky. An example is the victim of a swindle, the victim of someone else's financial failure, or a person who has suffered an uninsured catastrophe.

Bankruptcy may affect individual partners, and people who trade with unlimited liability. A topical example is the Lloyds of London "names". Bankruptcy can affect a director who has been guilty of wrongful trading and is personally liable for company debts. It can affect owners of limited companies who have given personal guarantees. This often happens to the owners of small businesses who find that it is the only way to get bank finance. For people like these the privileges of limited liability are sometimes illusory.

There are a lot of similarities between bankruptcy procedures and the compulsory winding up of companies. The assets are applied in the following order:

1. The costs of the bankruptcy.

2. Preferential creditors (if any).

3. Ordinary creditors (x pence in the pound). ◆

15

CREDIT AGENCIES

Although this chapter is entitled Credit Agencies its scope is a little wider and encompasses advice and services provided by outside credit and information specialists. The chapter starts with more general information and advice but goes on to discuss in detail the following five services:

- Provision of Purely Factual Information

- Details Beyond the Purely factual

- Recommendations and Ratings

- Collection Services

- Legal Action

There are over one hundred and fifty credit agencies in the UK. As you would expect their standards and costs vary quite a bit. It is therefore worth some care to select the one or two most likely to give the best results.

Some agencies have better records with particular trades or locations. Local and trade enquiries will probably produce one or two recommendations. If you have a large business, selling to many different trades across the country, you will probably do best with one of the large well-known names. Dun and Bradstreet is a very well known example. This might not give the best result in every individual case but it is likely to have a good average.

I recommend occasionally putting the same enquiry to more than one agency. You will be able to compare the results and form an opinion as to which is the more reliable and useful. This can hardly be done with collections and legal action as it would confuse the debtor. One can though put different cases to different agencies and see which does the best.

Some agencies ask for subscriptions on a regular basis and a guarantee of a certain number of enquiries. This is often financed by prepaying for a certain number of cases, usually in the form of a book of vouchers. Other agencies are happy to supply information on a one-off basis, and to charge accordingly. There has been some controversy over the charging methods of one or two agencies, and customers have complained that they have been misled into prepaying for more services than they need.

Do not make the mistake of thinking that credit agencies are infallible and if it is written down it must be right. A personal experience illustrates this very powerfully.

Five years ago I accepted an introductory offer of three free enquiries from an agency soliciting my business. I gave them the names of two new customers and an existing customer whom I thought I knew well. This customer had a long trading record with us. He sometimes paid a little slowly but I regarded him as safe. At the time of making the enquiry he owed us £80,000. The reply included the following:

'.....cause for concern. We recommend that no more than £500 credit be permitted and the position be reviewed in three months time'.

I took a deep breath then decided to ignore the report, taking the view that I knew more about my customer than the agency. My confidence was justified. Since then we have had five years of mutually profitable trading. At the time of writing their credit is £116,000 which does not worry me at all.

As with trade references you may know best about your existing customers. Credit Agencies are most useful when opening new accounts, though they have their uses with established accounts. My experience related above is highly damning to credit agencies, but it was only one agency on one occasion. Sometimes agencies are proved spectacularly right when events justify their caution. This can happen some time after the warning.

A problem for agencies is that few people remember the hundreds of times when they give a favourable report and the advice is sound. On the other hand their embarrassment is very public when a business fails shortly after having received a good recommendation. There must be a temptation to err on the side of caution.

Information usually comes by post which can be problem if speed of reply is important. For an extra fee a prompt response can be given by telex or more likely by fax. Several agencies have facilities for direct on line access to their data base. This is marvellous but do not be dazzled by the technology. The information is just as good or just as bad as if it had been despatched by carrier pigeon.

As with ordinary trade references you may get the best result if you ask a specific question relating to a specific sum. If you ask if a firm is good for £6,000 you may get a more useful response that if you just ask if their credit is good.

Never forget that you are interested in the speed at which an account is likely to be paid, as well as its safety. Many companies, particularly large companies, are safe as houses but rotten payers. It is interesting at my seminars to hear how the names of a few large companies are raised by the participants again and again. Their complaints relate to the abysmal slowness of payment rather than to the safety of the debt.

A credit enquiry may elicit rather a lot of information, some of which may duplicate what has been obtained from other sources. This may seem rather daunting but it is a "good fault" especially if the enquiry concerns a new account for which a large amount of credit is envisaged. One can disregard the superfluous and look on the duplication as useful confirmation.

The biggest problem likely to be encountered is insufficient or out of date information. Insufficient information is particularly likely to occur with businesses only having a short trading record. Accounts and other information may not yet be available at Companies House and the shortness of the trading record prohibits the obtaining of very useful references. In these circumstances you have to use your judgement and the information that you have.

Credit agencies sometimes put forward out of date information for established companies. This may be because they have not done a good job and obtained the latest filed information, or updated references and information from other sources. Of course established companies sometimes file accounts and other information late. Experience shows that companies that file information late may well not be a good credit risk. There are numerous exceptions but there is some truth in the belief that good news arrives quickly and bad news travels slowly.

Provision of Purely Factual Information

Examples of the sort of information available are

•   Exact trading name

•   Relationship with subsidiaries and parent company

•   Registered Charges

•   Details of Registered Office

•   Full details of directors and company secretary

•   Copies of audited accounts or key extracts from them

In the case of companies most of this information comes from Companies House. You can get it yourself either by applying to the main Cardiff office or to one of their other offices around the country. It is very likely to be uneconomic to do this yourself. Many agencies provide a first class service and they do so for a very reasonable fee. They do this due to economies of scale and anyone who has visited Companies House will have noticed numbers of earnest men and women conducting searches by the hundred. If the registration is not in England and Wales the other appropriate registration office must provide the information.

Details Beyond the Purely Factual

This means such things as trading references obtained by the agency. You may be told for example that two reliable sources spoke favourably of the subject and were happy to extend credit up to £20,000.

Recommendations and Ratings

Some agencies will give their own recommendation as to the credit worthiness of a subject. This may be in the form of a general comment or it may be specific to the sum put forward.

Some agencies operate a rating system and all businesses on their books are given a grade. Dun and Bradstreet are a notable example.

Ratings are very well established practice in the USA where certain changes in ratings receive wide publicity. At the time of writing one or two leading American banks have had their credit ratings downgraded by certain key agencies. This received very wide publicity and undoubtedly damaged the reputation of the banks. Arguably this was unfortunate because the banks in some cases had only been downgraded from extremely sound to just sound.

Collection Services

Some agencies will take over the running of a sales ledger and standard credit control procedures. Typically they send out a series of standard letters. It is claimed, and with some justification, that the name of a well known collection agency is likely to influence some customers towards paying promptly. They will feel that they are dealing with professionals unlikely to tolerate excuses. Furthermore they will not want to damage their credit standing in the eyes of the agency. Of course many customers are not influenced in this way, but some are.

As with factoring the best results are likely to be obtained with uncomplicated "clean debts". The reference back of queries and disputes can be a problem. It is another link in the chain and of course it costs money.

Legal Action

This may be a logical extension to the collection services, with the agency authorised to proceed to legal action if normal collection procedures do not succeed. Alternatively the agency may take on a case just at the point when legal proceedings are taken.

Legal action was covered in detail earlier in the book. Much of the advice related to the use of credit agencies as well as solicitors. Many credit agencies use solicitors and give a first class service. You should establish the basis of charging in advance and probably accept a "no payment no charge" arrangement. It is likely that you will still have to pay expenses. If you have a large uncomplicated debt with a high chance of success watch the percentage charges as it may result in a very high fee. You may be able to negotiate a separate arrangement or perhaps this one should be taken elsewhere. ◆

16

CREDIT INSURANCE

I have always followed the principle that it is wise to insure against catastrophe but not against misfortune, and I recommend this to anyone considering credit insurance. Such a person should first consider the size and spread of his debts. Secondly he should consider the effect on his business should the worst happen.

If there are no large debts but just a great number of individually small debts, it is probably a mistake to take out credit insurance. This is because, barring a series of events amounting to a statistical freak of unbelievable proportions, no combination of failures would have a catastrophic effect on the business. Over a period of time the premiums paid would probably add up to an amount similar to the money returned in the form of claims. As insurance companies have expenses and usually make a profit the premiums would probably be slightly larger than the claims.

If on the other hand one account is very large in relation to the total business, or there are several fairly large accounts, then credit insurance should be considered. A further factor is the resources of the business. If for example it is a soundly financed small subsidiary of a soundly financed large company, then perhaps even the failure of a major customer would not be regarded as a catastrophe. This line should not be taken lightly, but only as part of a carefully though out strategy concerning acceptable risk.

Money owing by customers is a very significant item on most Balance Sheets, but strangely this factor is sometimes overlooked when credit insurance is considered. Stock is routinely insured against perils such as fire and flood, and it is routinely insured against damage or theft whilst being transported. Does it not make sense to insure the debts after delivery? As stated elsewhere in this book there is no profit until the money is in the bank. The answer is that sometimes it makes sense and sometimes it does not. Each case should be considered on its merits.

Insurance companies generally want all debts insured, or at least whole sections. They do not want individual debts selected for insurance. This is a shame but of course the reason is obvious and they cannot be blamed. If it were possible to insure in this way customers would select those that they considered most at risk, and not insure those that they considered most safe.

Selection of Risks to be Insured

You normally have to insure all your accounts, or at least whole sectors of them. A friend of mine publishes textbooks which he sells to Local Education Authorities and also to bookshops. He regards the Local Education Authorities as slow payers but totally safe, and he does not insure this sector of his accounts He does though insure all his bookshop accounts.

It is possible in practice to insure just the large accounts by agreeing an "excess". This works on the same principle as car insurance where you might pay the first £100 of any claim.

Consider for example a business with a turnover of £500,000 a year. Let us assume that around £100,000 is owing at any one time. Let us also assume that there are three large customers who usually owe about £30,000 each and that the other £10,000 is made up of a dozen small accounts.

If an excess of £5,000 were agreed it would have the effect of in practice eliminating all but the three large accounts. In the event of a total loss a typical claim on one of the three large accounts would be for £25,000.

How Credit Insurance Works in Detail

Credit insurance is against tightly specified defined risks. These risks include such things as bankruptcy, company liquidation, and total disappearance of the debtor. Credit insurance does not cover slow payment and it does not cover disputes. It does not absolve the customer from the need to practise credit control procedures, collect the money, resolve disputes, and if necessary take legal action to secure payment.

Premium terms will be quoted for example as 30p per cent for 75% cover. This means that if annual turnover is £100,000 then the annual premium will be £300.

In the event of a total loss on an account owing £10,000 the pay out would be £7,500. If the failed customer pays 50p in the pound then the insurance payment will be £10,000 x 50% x 75% = £3,750. If any dividends from the debtor are made after the insurance pay out they will go 25% to the insurance company and 75% to its client.

The insurance company's small print will place an obligation on its client to take reasonable care when opening an account and reasonable care in conducting its business and operating the account. Credit insurance is not a licence to be reckless and cover can be invalidated in certain circumstances.

In the UK credit insurance is undertaken by specialist companies. This is because it is a specialist business and does not fit easily with other types of insurance business. They are owned by major insurance companies and reinsurance is provided by their owners. The major UK companies in the field are highly reputable and are generally considered to provide a good service. They do not operate exclusion clauses unreasonably.

It is only possible to insure sales to businesses, not sales to the public. The insurance company will normally insist that its client takes part of the risk. 75% cover to 90% cover is the normal range.

The cost of credit insurance will vary according to the business that it is in. Some sectors are rated more highly than others. Sectors such as small builders and small farmers are highly rated and premiums will be correspondingly high. As an extremely rough guide you might perhaps pay 0.5% of insured turnover for cover in a relatively good sector.

Working With Credit Insurance

Credit insurance should be regarded as complementary to good credit control. On no account should it be regarded as a substitute for it. Bad debts are bad for any business even if they are insured, and bad credit control may be punished in the following ways:

- A bad claims record may result in higher premiums

- Credit insurance does not give total cover. Part of the debt, perhaps just a small part, must be borne by the client.

- Bad credit control results in slow payment with the resultant interest costs to the business.

It is quite often possible to establish a very helpful relationship with one's credit insurance company. They succeed by being very good indeed at assessing risks and their opinions should be taken very seriously. Unlike credit agencies they back their judgment with their own money. They may be willing to give informal advice to an established customer and this is well worth pursuing if available.

If an account is refused the implications should be squarely faced. An insurance company makes money by accepting premiums. If it refuses premiums it does so for what it considers to be good reasons. If you accept business despite this warning you should have good reasons and be aware of the risk.

Insurance of Export Accounts

Credit insurance of export accounts is available from some commercial insurance companies, but the biggest provider is ECGD. This stands for Export Credit Guarantee Department and is part of the Department of Trade and Industry.

ECGD covers political risk, as well as the normal commercial risk. The term "political risk" includes war, payment embargoes by governments and many other risks. Premiums vary from country to country as well as by sector of the market. As I do not want to offend any of my readers I will not name any of the bad countries, but obviously certain developing countries have a much worse record than say Western Europe. This is reflected in the premiums.

Factoring

Non recourse factoring is a form of credit insurance. Factoring deserves, and gets, a chapter all to itself. ◆

17

FACTORING

Factoring is a way of getting next to immediate payment of debts. The factoring company will advance up to about 80% of invoices and it is therefore a massive boost to cash flow.

As well as providing the payment the factoring company will provide administrative support. It will maintain the sales ledger and operate credit control procedures for the client. If the arrangement is for non-recourse factoring (see below) the factoring company will give 100% protection against bad debts. Furthermore it is normally willing to give advice to its clients on the standing of customers, good credit procedures, and so on.

There are several variations of factoring and it can be divided into the following three broad categories.

Non-Recourse Factoring

This gives 100% protection against bad debts on transactions accepted by the factoring company. The factoring company will maintain the sales ledger and look after the credit control function.

The existence of factoring is usually disclosed to the customer who is asked to pay directly to the factoring company. Alternatively it may be undisclosed, and if this is the case the client makes payments to the factoring company as money comes in from its customers.

Recourse Factoring

This operates in the same way as non-recourse factoring, but the factor does not take the bad debt risk. A specified time is agreed and if payment has not been received by the due date then the client must reimburse the factor with the amount advanced.

Invoice Discounting

This is an advance of a certain proportion of monies outstanding on the sales ledger, and secured by the debts in the sales ledger. As the total balance on the sales ledger goes up and down, payments are made one way or the other.

Invoice Discounting is technically not factoring at all, but is included in this chapter because some of its features are similar. It is purely a secured financial advance with no administrative help or maintenance of the sales ledger. The amount advanced is an agreed percentage of the sales ledger.

Invoice Discounting is the fastest growing sector in factoring.

Factoring is not as expensive as is sometimes supposed. Interest is payable on the sum advanced and is calculated on a day to day basis whilst the loan is outstanding. The interest rate is typically 2% to 3% over bank base rates.

In addition a fee is paid and this is a percentage of the sum advanced. This fee will vary according to credit risk and the sector of the customer. As a rough guide the fee will vary between 0.75% and 2.5%. As with credit insurance certain sectors are loaded because of their high risk and in some cases cover may be hard to obtain. For example the fee is likely to be high if the customer is a small builder.

Factoring is only available on business to business sales. It is not available if you sell to the public. Factoring companies are likely to want annual turnover of at least £80,000 from each of their clients (this is factoring companies' clients not individual customers of clients). Businesses smaller than this are not likely to be of interest to them.

Some factors specialise in export sales. Their services have all the usual benefits but clients are likely to be attracted to the prospect of simplifying their procedures on export sales.

As we know collection of export debts can be troublesome and time consuming.

The image of factoring has two strands. On the one hand there is a certain feeling that one would only go to a factor as one of the sources of credit of last resort. This is probably rooted in the attitudes and circumstances of the past. My own view is that this is nonsense and if there ever was any truth in it this is no longer the case. Several of my own suppliers factor their debts and it does not worry me at all.

The more favourable image is the one promoted by the factoring companies. It is of a professional, regulated, modern business giving a good service and providing a legitimate source of finance to its clients. This is close to my own view, but of course readers will have their own opinions.

Factoring has seen a great expansion in recent years and this trend seems set to continue. It is found that it is a good way to unlock some of the value of debts tied up in the sales ledger. This is always useful, but is particularly helpful in times of difficult trading.

The following are my views on the advantages and disadvantages of factoring.

Advantages of Factoring

The overwhelming reason for factoring is the boost to cash flow from next to immediate payment of invoices. It is now recognised as a main source of finance.

It is sometimes claimed that the disclosed involvement of a factor will increase the likelihood of prompt payment by customers. This is because customers are likely to think that they are dealing with professionals unlikely to be swayed by excuses.

As with all services standards vary, but the factor is likely to provide an efficient computerised sales ledger, and an efficient collection service.

Factors may provide a source of advice, encouragement, and credit information.

Non-recourse factoring provides 100% protection against specified bad debts and is an extension of credit insurance covered in the last chapter.

Disadvantages of Factoring

Costs are not as high as is sometimes supposed but nothing is for nothing. It has to be paid for.

The factor can only provide an efficient sales ledger service if it is provided with accurate, timely information. It cannot solve disputes and it may be an unnecessary link in the chain between supplier and customer. For this reason it is most suited to clean uncomplicated debts. The computer industry has a catchword GIGO which stands for "Garbage In equals Garbage Out". The same is true of sales ledgers. Conversely the involvement of an outsider can force a client to solve disputes and improve its procedures.

Some people believe that a supplier may be devalued in the eyes of its customer if it uses a factor. I have already said that there is not too much truth in this and in some cases the involvement is not disclosed anyway.

The factor will want first call on the trade debts as security for the advances that it gives. This will probably reduce the value of the security available to a bank which will probably have a fixed and floating charge on the assets. Money available from the bank will probably therefore be reduced, thus diminishing (but not eliminating) the main reason for factoring debts in the first place. The reduction in bank finance is unlikely to be one for one, and a more cooperative attitude may be found if the factoring company is a subsidiary of the bank.

It is neither an advantage nor a disadvantage but a fact of life, that the money unlocked by factoring can only be released once. If the sales ledger has a more or less constant total of £1,000,000 then £800,000 may be released by factoring. This sum may of course be partially offset by a reduction in the bank overdraft facility.

No more can be released unless the value of sales and of the sales ledger increases. If business drops off and the value of the sales ledger reduces, a net repayment to the factor must be made. This may be stating the obvious but sometimes it is necessary to do just that.

If a company's accounting and control systems have not kept up with the business there may be a case for getting the administrative help of a factor. Nevertheless I would still pose the question "why pay someone for doing what you can do yourself?" For most people the reason for factoring is that it releases money tied up in the business.　◆

18

LESS USUAL COLLECTION METHODS

It is normal to start the collecting process by sending out statements. There is a view that time and money should be saved by dispensing with statements, as some customers disregard them. It is certainly true that some will be disregarded but I am firmly of the opinion that statements should be sent. Many customers do use them and the benefits of sending them outweigh the costs.

In the great majority of cases the collection methods used are letters or telephone calls or a combination of the two. Standard letters are practical when relatively large numbers of debts have to be collected. Telephone collection is generally considered to be especially effective, but constraints of time and money inevitably restrict its use. When the ledger consists of a small number of large debts it may be possible to ring every customer as necessary. This certainly gets good results.

After letters and telephone calls have failed, or after an acceptable period of time has elapsed, it is usual to move on to stronger methods. This usually means suspending supplies (if orders are still being placed), issuing a final warning letter, then as the ultimate step taking legal action.

These methods are the right ones to use in most cases and they succeed in most cases. This is why a significant part of the book covers these subjects. However, it is worth a brief mention of certain other collection methods and this chapter puts forward several for consideration.

Some are rather light hearted but they may trigger some useful ideas. Others are of much more general application and it may well be that they will be very relevant.

Personal Visits

This is normally the most effective collection method of all as it puts psychological pressure on the customer. It is much more difficult to make excuses when there is a living person in the same room. Some excuses cannot be made because they can be seen to be lies. It is difficult to say there is no-one to sign the cheque when the appropriate cars are in the car park and can be seen from the office window.

Other excuses can still be made but you are much more likely to know that they are excuses, and the customer will know that you know. Even if you do not take a cheque away you are very likely to have a good idea of the truth. This means that you can take the next appropriate step, perhaps legal action, much more quickly.

There are benefits to dropping in unexpectedly but it is usually best to say in advance that you will be calling. This gives the customer the time to get the cheque ready and to prepare any matters that he wants to raise. It does give him time to prepare his excuses, but if he does this you will probably realise what is happening.

An often forgotten benefit of a personal visit is the saving of one or two days interest due to the post. This is particularly valuable if the amount is large and the caller takes a bank paying in book with him.

Personal visits are expensive and time consuming. Unless you have just a few large accounts it is necessary to be very selective with the visits and to make each one effective.

There are different views about asking salesmen to collect money. They are the people who frequently visit customers and it may be practical for them to collect, whereas it may be a physical impossibility for the credit controller to get round. On the other hand salesmen are employed to sell and it is what they are trained to do. Their contacts are probably with buyers and not with accounts offices. They may dislike collecting, may not be very good at it, and it may reduce the sales effort.

I find it difficult to generalise about salesmen collecting. I have known many excellent salesmen who made terrible collectors. In the interests of them, their employers, and their customers, it was definitely a mistake to ask them to collect. On the other hand I have known salesmen who managed to do the trick wonderfully.

I strongly recommend cultivating an atmosphere where all staff visiting a customer look out for an opportunity to bring back a cheque. This does not mean that it has to be the over-riding priority, just that everyone is aware that their best efforts would be appreciated. A word in the right ear can do wonders. Maybe a joke can be made of it. Perhaps the visitor can say something like "They won't let me back if I have not got a cheque with me. They're going to board up my office and leave me in the corridor".

There are often opportunities for an accounts department to ask in advance for a cheque to be ready for a salesman or other caller to collect. This takes the pressure off the salesman in that he just has to say that he believes that there is something for collection, and does not have to do any detailed negotiating. Many of the benefits of personal visits will accrue, and the customer should feel some obligation to have a cheque ready.

EDI

This stands for Electronic Data Interchange. As the name implies it is a process of linking two computers. All sorts of information may be transmitted in this way, but in the context of credit control we are most interested in linking the invoicing and sales ledger accounting of the seller with the purchase ledger accounting of the buyer.

This means that an invoice is raised simultaneously in the offices of the buyer and seller. Subject to appropriate checks it is then entered into the purchase ledger of the buyer. This cuts out postal delays and the simultaneous matching of information simplifies checking and accounting.

EDI is a very big subject and its use is expanding rapidly. There are obvious advantages in efficiency for all parties and major companies are increasingly insisting on its use.

EDI should aid the credit control effort. The purchaser is unlikely to allow you to take the money directly from him without his say so, even though it may be technically possible. It is possible that he will allow you to take it subject to his checks and approval. At the least the increased efficiency should make it easier to get payment.

Fax And Telex

Fax and telex are methods of transmitting hard copies of messages directly into customers' offices. Additionally the use of fax, which is gaining ground at the expense of the telex, enables one to copy a document (such as an invoice) directly to a customer. These marvels are only available if the customer subscribes to the necessary equipment. More and more customers at home and abroad are doing so.

A credit control message sent by fax or telex has novelty value that makes it stand out from the numerous similar messages sent by letter. The receiver may subconsciously associate it with something urgent. Of course as the use of fax and telex increases, this effect reduces. I receive numerous such messages. Some of them are unsolicited advertising, and I treat them much less seriously than formerly.

They have the advantage of immediate transmission and the sender can be sure that the message has arrived. Unlike a telephone call, the message is put into print and a permanent record is issued.

I recommend the intelligent use of fax and telex to send credit control messages. I particularly recommend the use of fax to send copies of missing documents. This should be routine as it saves postal delays.

In passing, Customs & Excise require that a VAT invoice should be an original copy, or if faxed should be certified by a signature as a true copy of an original. This need not worry us unduly and I speak from personal experience. Problems are most unlikely and one can always ask a supplier for a hard copy in the unlikely event of being asked to do so by Customs & Excise.

The Use of Humour

Many years ago I was responsible for a rather inefficient purchase ledger department. There was no deliberate policy of delaying payments to suppliers but due to inefficiency it quite often happened. One day I received a personal letter from a supplier asking me to sort out the problems on his account. The envelope contained two copies of the same letter. One was marked "For the attention of the Left Hand" and the other was marked "For the attention of the Right Hand".

My first reaction was to fall about laughing, and the second was to feel embarrassed that anyone could show me up in that way. I did immediately sort out the account and a cheque for the correct amount was posted that night. It was a high risk strategy because it might have offended me and made an enemy, but the use of humour achieved the desired effect.

You may well be able to tell a funny story like the above, and you will almost certainly be aware that a humorous touch can sometimes unlock doors that normal systems do not breach. Official jokes are a contradiction in terms but you should keep in mind the potential of humour. Of course there are more opportunities if you get to know the customers. You will get to know who is likely to respond, and who is best treated in a serious manner.

When a customer sends an unexpectedly small cheque you could ring and thank him for the down payment. I did this recently and a cheque for the remainder was posted the same day. I knew the customer and he saw the joke and the point behind it. This is an example of the effective use of humour.

Publicity

All businesses fear bad publicity. Press reports of things such as safety pins in the baby food can and do cost the manufacturers vast amounts of money. This is true whether the safety pins were put there accidentally, deliberately, or even not at all.

The threat of publicity may provoke a slow payer into improving his record. It will obviously jeopardize the chance of future business and probably end such business. It is such a powerful weapon that one should consider very carefully whether one is morally justified in using it. One should also of course consider whether one is legally justified in using it and your attention is drawn to the section on Harassment at the end of this chapter. Finally, it is wise to be sure that you have nothing to lose from bad publicity directed in return.

I first thought deeply about publicity when I worked for a subsidiary of Lord Grade's Associated Communications Corporation Ltd. At the Annual General Meeting a shareholder asked why Ivor Novello's bust had been removed from the foyer of the London Palladium, and asked that it be found and returned. The press took up the story and the resulting hullabaloo forced out the stories that the company had hoped to promote as a result of the meeting.

A more vicious example of the same thing occurred at the 1991 Annual General Meeting of the Midland Bank. A shareholder compared the Chairman's salary with that of General Norman Schwarzkopf who had just led the victorious forces in the Gulf War.

I think I can guarantee that a public company would consider its position carefully if it received notice that a small supplier had bought a few shares and intended to ask the following question at the Annual General Meeting:

> "Would Sir Wilfred please accept the congratulations of shareholders on his appointment as Chairman of the Government Committee to examine the difficulties of small businesses in Wales. Would Sir Wilfred please explain why his company has delayed for over six months paying £15,000 due to David Lloyd Evans Ltd, resulting in two redundancies in that small Welsh company."

Stickers

These are either serious or humorous messages stuck on statements to increase their impact. I am very sceptical about their effectiveness but I stop short of saying that they have no effect at all. A simple message might say something like "Overdue - Please Remit".

They are not likely to have much influence on a large company but just might make some difference to a small customer. They might make your statement stand out from the pile.

Direct Debits and Standing Orders

A standing order is initiated by the payer's bank. A direct debit is initiated by the beneficiary who claims payment from the payer's bank. Direct debits may be fixed amounts or for variable amounts. Direct debits may only be used by organisations authorised to do so by the banks and of course the authority of the customer to be debited must also be obtained.

Standing orders and especially direct debits are very attractive payment methods for suppliers. It is more difficult to see why customers should agree to make payment in this way and I tend to resist when asked to do so.

A reason for doing so is because the supplier may give an inducement. One example is local authorities who permit payment of rates over a period if payment is by this method. Insurance companies often allow payment by instalments if this method is used.

The advantages for the seller are great and it is worth considerable efforts to persuade customers to use the system. It may be worth inducements to get them to do so. Sellers in a very strong position sometimes use force majeure to get customers to do it. Effectively customers are told that they must pay in this way or not deal at all. This might seem hard but as an advisor on credit control I cannot blame suppliers for exploiting the strength that they have.

Telegraphic Transfers

One thinks of Telegraphic Transfers as a way of remitting money overseas. Inland Telegraphic Transfers achieve same day transfer of cleared funds within this country. Again there are obvious advantages for suppliers and I recommend that you ask for it in appropriate circumstances. It is often used where payment is required before goods are released. The supply of motor cars is one such example.

Credit Cards

One thinks of credit cards in relation to the general public but there is no reason why sales to businesses should not use them. Individual businessmen carry credit cards and are capable of using them for company purchases. This is particularly true of cards such as American Express where there are high limits or no limits.

An acquaintance of mine exports services and makes a lot of semi-cold calls in foreign countries. He gets most of his payments in this way, finding the sureness and convenience well worth the percentage that he pays to the credit card companies.

Blacklisting

Earlier in this book I posed the question "What are your sanctions?" In most cases the answer is suspension of supplies followed by legal action. A threat or the actuality of appropriate blacklisting can be very effective indeed. A formal or informal pooling of information by suppliers within the same trade has great benefits for them all. This is often done through the medium of a trade association. The threat of inclusion in the blacklist may persuade a customer to be reasonable.

Consideration under this heading can also be given to a threat to report the customer to his own professional organisation or trade association. The effectiveness of this will vary according to the customer, the trade, and the standards of the professional association or trade association.

Elsewhere in this book I told of a threat to report a slow paying solicitor to the Law Association. I rather suspect that the Law Association would not have helped but the threat alone achieved the desired result.

Harassment

I finish the chapter with this because you must not do it, and you may get into severe trouble if you do.

Like most people I am glad that laws exist to prevent wives and children of debtors being shamed more than is going to happen anyway. I am glad that laws exist to enforce certain standards, and to give sanctuary in a private home. Nevertheless, I sometimes feel a certain sympathy for potential harassers. There are a number of crooks who exploit suppliers, sometimes small businesses who can ill afford to lose the money. In these circumstances a series of telephone calls at 3 am can be very tempting. But do not do it please.

There is a line that must not be crossed. Various Acts of Parliament make it illegal, particularly the Administration of Justice Act 1970. So please take all the legal steps explained in this book and stop short of anything illegal. ◆

19

WARNING SIGNS - DANGER IMMINENT

You will probably have seen several humorous lists of danger signs. They tend to be along the lines of fountains in the entrance hall, new offices for the accounts staff, and personalised number plates on the Chairman's Rolls Royce. As well as being highly entertaining they often contain a core of truth.

The points listed are usually based on expenditure above the means of the company, diversification away from the core business that made the company successful and management doing things other than running the business. The corporate graveyard is full of companies whose Chief Executives received too many awards and served on too many committees.

It is very important that you get warning of an impending disaster. You may be able to limit or perhaps even eliminate your exposure. Warning signs may be obtained from accounts though they may only be available too late to be of much use. You should get warning from your credit agency if you use one.

The following is a practical list designed to trigger alarm bells. In my experience the first two points are the most important.

Any Change for the Worse in the Payments Pattern

This is a key sign. As well as a bad payments record you are looking for a deteriorating record. A customer paying in 90 days instead of the usual 60 is more worrying than one who has always taken 90 days and still docs. This cannot be hidden as the information is always available in the sales ledger.

Something In The Voice

This is extremely hard to describe but you will know what is meant. It is an unusual tone of voice, unusual formality, nervousness, and so on. It will be most readily noticed when you are familiar with the speaker and have spoken to him many times. It might be termed information gleaned from a sixth sense.

An experienced collector would probably say that this has alerted him more often than any of the other signs. You should usually trust your instincts, or at least trust them enough to make further enquiries.

More Than One Mistake On A Cheque

Hercule Poirot said that one mistake is a mistake but that two mistakes are a clue. To err is human but to do it again is suspicious.

You will be familiar with customers who forget to sign cheques or send cheques with differing words and figures. Occasionally it is accidental but often it is a ploy to gain time. The motive may be to save interest, but it may be that the customer is having difficulties and funds are not available. If it keeps happening it is wise to make what checks you can.

Always Referred To Someone Else

Most people hate telling lies or misleading people, especially if it is to a person that they know and like. In particular the junior staff may feel, probably correctly, that the problem is not their fault so why should they cover up for the boss. Rather than do so they may keep referring the call to each other or to a senior person who never seems to be there.

If you keep being passed from person to person there may be bad news at the end of it. This point should be considered with "Something in the Voice". They often go together.

People Never Ring Back

This is similar to the heading above, especially if it is a person who is normally helpful.

Cheque Just Never Comes

The cheque is in the post or will be sent now. Its a poor excuse and you should respond as advised in Chapter 9 which dealt with excuses.

It may be an attempt to gain time for its own sake, or it may be an unethical attempt to save interest. Most worryingly of all it may show an inability to pay. I once waited a very long time for a cheque said to have been sent. It never did arrive but I did eventually get a copy of the customer's letter of complaint to the Post Office.

People Avoiding You - Always In Meetings

Given the way that most businesses are run people often really are in meetings, but only up to a point. Avoiding speaking to someone asking for payment is one of the classic signs of trouble. It is a way of buying time.

High Staff Turnover

A business that is having problems paying its bills and is heading for trouble may be frequently replacing staff. This is because the working atmosphere is probably not happy, and because the insiders want to secure their futures.

Empty Shelves

This happens when other suppliers are refusing deliveries and it is a very bad sign. It will mean less bills to pay but it will probably indicate reduced future revenues which will make the problem worse.

It could also of course mean seasonal variations, or a positive drive to improve the situation by eliminating overtrading or trading in unprofitable lines.

Unnaturally Large Orders

Large orders are usually good news. Very large orders from a customer who may have problems may be very bad news indeed. If you are unlucky and careless you may have a large bad debt, your normal business plus the extra orders as well.

You should ask yourself if your customer has increased his order to you because he cannot get supplies elsewhere.

Late Accounts

Financial journalists have come to be wary when publication of results is delayed, whatever the stated reason. More often than not the figures will be bad when they are eventually published.

Creative Accountancy

An examination of back accounts of companies that have failed almost always reveals that the directors have resorted to creative accountancy, and sometimes plain misleading accountancy. Auditors sometimes accept the practices, and sometimes say that the accounts are true and fair but ensure that the reader has the benefit of a note to the accounts disclosing the practices. Unfortunately the notes may be obscure, perhaps may not be read and will probably be only significant to the financially sophisticated.

Examples of creative accountancy are the unreasonable capitalisation of Research and Development costs and the unreasonable capitalisation of interest in building or construction contracts.

Press Comment

The laws of libel make if difficult for the press to voice their suspicions openly. Instead they often draw their readers attention to impending problems in a sort of code. At the time of writing, alert newspaper readers are noticing coded messages about a major British company. Credit Controllers might do well to ponder the implications and look to their defences.

Despite all this please do not always believe the press when they are wise after the event. The city and the press "knew" that Barlow Clowes was dodgy and they all said so in print. The city and the press "knew" that the Bank of Credit and Commerce International was going to go. Nonsense! Many of the people who say it now knew no such thing.

Round Sum Cheques

Round sum cheques on account are a very obvious indication of possible problems. They may be said to be due to staff problems, or problems reconciling the account, or an attempt to make a fair payment pending resolution of a dispute. All this may sometimes be true, but do not overlook the chance that money is short and that this is the true reason. Do of course take and bank round sum cheques because they are better than nothing. But do take time to consider the possible implications.

None of the above points should be taken as proof that serious trouble is pending. They may all have an innocent explanation. However, you should take them seriously and if you notice two or more you should be even more cautious.

When your suspicions are aroused you should make whatever independent checks are reasonable and available. This is a time when a credit reference agency can be invaluable, and it is a time to place one or two shrewd telephone calls. ◆

20

BAD DEBTS

It would be nice to think that this chapter is being read only as a matter of academic interest. Unfortunately this would not be very realistic. Any company with more than just a few credit customers is likely to have at least an occasional bad debt.

Bad debts are inevitable for a company that makes significant sales on credit particularly if made directly to the public. Managers of such a company should budget a certain percentage of sales as a bad debt reserve. Having done this they should take strenuous steps to keep the number of bad debts as small as realistically possible, and to minimise their losses. A company giving credit to just a few customers may avoid bad debts at least for a time. When one does occur it can be a nasty shock, especially if it is unexpected or the amount is large.

As a matter of practical management it is usually necessary to balance a wish to boost sales with a wish to keep bad debts to a minimum. Exactly how this is done and where the balance is struck is a matter for judgement in individual cases.

The common understanding of a bad debt is that it is what happens when a customer goes bust. Common understanding is wrong. A better definition of a bad debt is that it happens when either

a customer cannot pay

OR

a customer will not pay and you are unable or unwilling to take the necessary steps to force him to pay.

Furthermore the amount of the bad debt may be reduced by any VAT that can be reclaimed, by any stock that may be recovered, by any dividend that may be paid by the debtor, and by any amount covered by credit insurance.

Having made that clear the rest of this chapter deals with what happens when a customer "goes bust". The following are the steps that you can take to protect your position and minimise the loss.

Use The Full Extent Of Your Terms

This was discussed in Chapter 11. In a business relationship it is quite normal for a supplier not to invoice every last penny that a strict interpretation of the contract would enable him to bill. This may be because he intends to waive it in the interests of the long term relationship.

When a customer goes bust there is not going to be any long term relationship. You should get the short term benefits by billing everything that you can. The possibilities will vary from case to case but the following are among the things to consider.

- Does the contract entitle you to charge interest on this or previous late payments?

- Are there any penalty clauses that could be invoked?

- Is it possible to charge for ancillary items such as travel or training?

- It may be contractually possible to raise late invoices for old business as well as invoices for current items.

A customer's insolvency or liquidation may lead to a payment of x pence in the pound. Quite often there is not enough to fully satisfy the secured creditors and the preferential creditors. When this happens the payment to ordinary creditors will be nil pence in the pound and increasing the amount of the debt will not achieve anything.

On the other hand it will increase the return if there is some dividend. For example consider a debt of £20,000 where there is a dividend of 50p in the pound. The dividend would be £10,000 and the bad debt £10,000. Now let us assume that ancillary invoicing increases the debt to £22,000 and as a result the dividend drops to 49p in the pound. The dividend would be £10,780, an improvement of £780.

Liquidators, bankrupts, and others sometimes bitterly complain about the practices that I am advocating. It is possible to understand their point of view, particularly when a deficit turns out to be much larger than accounts indicated. However, suppliers facing a bad debt have rights too. The position is usually a competitive one and the gain of one supplier is at the expense of all the other suppliers. The individual debtor only suffers if there is personal liability.

I am of course advocating the invoicing only of what is legitimately and contractually due. Anything beyond this would be dishonest and should not be considered.

Consider Enforcing Retention Of Title

This was explained fully in the chapter on Conditions of Sale. The following is an outline of the conditions that must exist in order for a retention of title clause to be effective:

- Your terms must apply

- You must be able to relate specific stock to specific unpaid invoices

- You must give credit in full (including VAT) for stock taken back

- You can only repossess by agreement or by invoking the law. You do not have the right of forcible removal

- You cannot take goods that have been mixed with other goods or altered. For example you can only take leather that you have supplied, not shoes made from that leather.

- You can only repossess from your customer, not from someone who has bought from your customer in good faith.

Careful thought should be given before an attempt is made to enforce a retention of title clause. You have the job of satisfying the Liquidator that your claim is a sound one and you have the administrative job of identifying your stock. You have the job of loading the stock, transporting it, and putting it back into your warehouse. All this will be at your expense.

You must give full value for what you take even though it might not still be worth as much. The stock may have lost value if it is soiled or if it is a fashion item such as dresses.

You would in any case have recovered the VAT on the recovered stock and the apparent saving will not be quite so large for this reason.

I am not saying that you should not repossess stock if entitled to do so. Usually you should. I am saying that all points should be considered and that the benefits may not be quite so large as hoped for.

Liquidators and Receivers are in practice likely to be sceptical about retention of title claims, and in particular they will probably make you prove that your terms governed the contact. Just exhibiting a copy of your terms on an unsigned document will probably not be good enough.

They will have access to legal advice and will make you prove your claim. This is fair enough and if you think that your claim is a good one you should be prepared to do so.

You should let the Liquidator or Receiver know that you have a retention of title claim as soon as you hear that one has been appointed. This will probably result in an annoying period when not very much happens. Then you are likely to be given a form asking for information about the claim. Some of the requested information will be relevant, and some will seem irrelevant. Quite possibly some of it will seem impertinent. This will be because the form has been designed to cover all eventualities, rather than with your particular circumstances in mind.

You should send in the form as soon as possible, having completed all the reasonable parts and some of the mildly unreasonable parts. It is a good idea to write to the Liquidator or Receiver warning them not to move, damage, or intermingle stock that is the subject of your claim. You should also do this if there is a delay in sending the form to you.

Liquidators and Receivers are often reasonable people and they do a difficult job. You will usually get the right result if you have a good case and you make it in the proper way. If you have a doubtful case it might be worth putting it forward anyway.

Do not tolerate an unreasonable delay or the rejection of what you think is a good case. Liquidators and Receivers hate litigation. As well as my own experience on this point I have the word of a Licensed Insolvency Practitioner. If your case is a good one the threat of legal action will almost certainly achieve the right result. If your claim is a bad one it probably will not make any difference.

Get Back The VAT

If you charge VAT you should at least get this back. The rules for VAT bad debt relief changed in 1990 and the two systems are running side by side.

Invoices dated up to July 26 1990

Bad debt relief is only available in the case of formal liquidation or bankruptcy, and provided that the necessary certificate has been obtained. Relief is available from the date of the certificate and may be claimed in the next VAT return.

Invoices dated after July 1 1989

Bad Debt relief is available when the invoice has been unpaid for one year and has been fully written off in the accounts. This means fully written off in internal accounts records. It is not necessary to wait until signed accounts are available.

Invoices dated between July 1 1989 and July 26 1990

You may choose to claim relief either under the old rules or the new rules. It is normally best to claim under the new rules.

The changes were announced in Mr Major's 1990 Budget but with a delay of 2 years. Mr Lamont shortened the wait to 1 year in his 1991 Budget. July 26 1990 is the date of Royal Assent to the 1990 Finance Act.

Customs and Excise require that proper records are kept. If any payment is ever received after bad debt relief has been given the correct VAT proportion must subsequently be paid over to Customs and Excise.

There is an obvious advantage in writing off a debt that has become a year old, and writing it back if it is ever paid. As a practical matter it may be worth doing this instead of one less than a year old, even though the prospects for the newer one may not be so good. Certainly specific write-offs should be made rather than the creation of a general bad debt reserve.

Personal Liability

If a person is trading in his own name without forming a limited company he will be personally liable for the debts. The same applies to partnerships where the individual partners will have what is known as joint and several liability. This means that the personal assets of all partners are available to pay the debts of the partnership.

The ultimate cost of personal liability is bankruptcy and either alone or with other creditors you may take steps to make the debtor bankrupt. In practice this is often not done, particularly if the debtor's conduct has not been too bad and if the deficit is not too large. Human feelings sometimes prevent the steps being taken, but one must also consider the costs of bankruptcy and the realistic prospects of dividends from the bankrupt.

The owners of a limited liability company do not normally have personal liability for the debts. However, in practice they often give personal guarantees to banks or other lenders. It is open to a supplier to demand personal guarantees in support of supplies to a limited company. It is not often done and is likely to be strongly resisted. Nevertheless it is an option which should sometimes be considered.

It sometimes happens that an individual trades as a company whilst leading suppliers to believe that he is trading with personal liability. For example his notepaper and other stationery may not disclose the existence of a company as is required by law. In these circumstances you may well succeed in holding the trader personally liable for the company debts.

Directors may be disqualified from acting as a director for a specified number of years, and may be personally liable for company debts, if their conduct falls below a certain standard. In particular this may happen if they carry on trading when they know, or ought to know, that there is no reasonable prospect of avoiding insolvent liquidation.

Licensed Insolvency Practitioners have an obligation to make a report on the conduct of directors With this in mind they often ask creditors if there are any matters which they wish to bring to their attention.

In practice it is rare for a director to be made personally liable for the debts of a limited company and a high standard of proof is required.

Monitor What Happens

If the liquidation is expected to be an insolvent one the proceedings will be under the control of the creditors. The initial meeting of creditors will appoint the Liquidator who will make reports to creditors during the liquidation. A committee of the creditors will keep an eye on the liquidation throughout its progress.

The notice convening the meeting of creditors gives each creditor an opportunity to attend and vote. The notice will be accompanied by a form of proxy which you may use if you wish. In order to cast a vote at the meeting of creditors you must send in the form certifying that you are a creditor.

You may decide to ignore the whole thing, opting to take pot luck on what happens and just banking any dividend cheques that ultimately arrive. For many small creditors this is a sensible attitude to take. You must though take the trouble to supply proof of the debt in order to take part in any distribution ultimately made.

You may decide to attend the meeting of creditors and cast your vote personally. Alternatively you may decide to use the proxy form and have someone represent you. It is not a good idea to sign the form in blank and return it. This is because your vote will then be cast by the chairman of the meeting who will probably be a director of the failed company. Now that Liquidators have to be Licensed Insolvency Practitioners there are fewer abuses. Nevertheless, you will probably want to resist the idea of the directors choosing the Liquidator.

You may be able to get most of the advantages of attending without actually doing so. This can be done by appointing a representative of a major accounting firm to represent you. He will give you an independent report and cast your vote for you, either using his judgement or in accordance with your instructions. What is more he will probably do this without charging you a fee.

He will do this not because he is a kindly man, though he may well be, but because by attending the meeting he hopes to attract work to his insolvency department. If you use the services of a large accounting firm you can approach them directly. If you do not do so your solicitor, accountant, or other professional adviser will probably be pleased to make a recommendation and introduction.

And Finally - Learn the Lessons

A bad debt represents the ultimate failure. Do not brood too much because an occasional bad debt is inevitable for most who supply on credit. Nevertheless, you should monitor both the number of bad debts and the amounts lost. Neither should be higher than an acceptable percentage given all the circumstances. When a bad debt occurs you should ask some searching questions:

•   Was it bad luck or bad judgement?

•   Was the amount of the debt bigger than it should have been?

•   Would any reasonable steps have averted the bad debt?

•   Are there any lessons to be learned?

Note that you are only looking for reasonable steps, not something unreasonable and unrealistically restrictive.

Finally, you might like to ask yourself if anyone is to blame and do they need some advice. If you yourself are to blame then learn the lessons and keep quiet.   ◆

About The Publisher

Hawksmere Ltd. publishes a range of business, finance and project management titles, all of them readable, usable, concise and practical.

Hawksmere also runs over 250 one and two-day seminars, mainly in the UK. Principal subject areas covered are:

• Business Strategy and development • Finance • Marketing and public relations • Pensions and insurance • Business and Commercial Law • Property • Tax and accountancy • Entertainment Law • Engineering and Project management.

In addition Hawksmere runs in-house training programmes for many client companies.

For further information call 071-824 8257 or write Hawksmere at the address below.

HAWKSMERE

Hawksmere Limited, 12-18 Grosvenor Gardens
Belgravia, London SW1W 0DH
Telephne 071-824 8257, Fax 071-730 4293